FINDING YOUR PLACE IN GOD'S GREAT STORY

PAUL BASDEN & JIM JOHNSON

HARVEST HOUSE PUBLISHERS
EUGENE, OREGON

Cover design by Dugan Design Group

Interior design by KUHN Design Group

Cover illustrations © artinspiring (plant), juliars (phone), Anton Shaparenko (coffee cup) / Adobe Stock; all other illustrations by Devon Laird

For bulk, special sales, or ministry purchases, please call 1 (800) 547-8979.
Email: Customerservice@hhpbooks.com

M This logo is a federally registered trademark of the Hawkins Children's LLC. Harvest House Publishers, Inc., is the exclusive licensee of this trademark.

Finding Your Place in God's Great Story
Copyright © 2023 by Paul Basden and Jim Johnson
Published by Harvest House Publishers
Eugene, Oregon 97408
www.harvesthousepublishers.com

ISBN 978-0-7369-8121-7 (pbk.)
ISBN 978-0-7369-8122-4 (eBook)

Library of Congress Control Number: 2022933254

Printed in the United States of America

22 23 24 25 26 27 28 29 30 / VP / 10 9 8 7 6 5 4 3 2 1

To the Preston Trail family.

It's been a privilege and joy to bring
messages from God's Word to you
for the past twenty years.

CONTENTS

THE POWER OF STORY

Star Wars.

The Avengers.

Harry Potter.

Lord of the Rings.

X-Men.

Other than making a boatload of money, what do these film franchises have in common?

They all tell stories. Exciting stories. Thrilling stories. Addictive stories.

Once you get started watching, you can't stop. That's the power of a good story.

Story is all the rage these days. Authors and musicians and screenwriters all aim to craft the best stories they can so that we will read their books, listen to their songs, and watch their movies. With storytelling as a model, expert consultants can teach you how to improve your business presentations and increase your market share.[1] The power of story seems to know no end.

But story is not just something you read on a page or watch in a theater. Story is also something you live. You see, *you* have a story. Everyone you know has a story. Even God has a story. And that's the premise of this book.

GOD HAS A STORY

Have you ever thought about how friendships are formed? They usually start when you say to someone, "Tell me about yourself." Then after listening a while, you return the favor. Along the way, you come to understand one another. When you know someone's story, you know *them*. When they know your story, they know *you*.

This is true in the spiritual realm as well. Suppose you were to ask God, "Would you please tell me about yourself?" God might reply, "Sit down. It's going to take a while. Are you listening? Do you really want to know me? If so, here's my story." That divine story is found in only one place.

GOD'S STORY IS TOLD IN THE BIBLE

When you hear the word "Bible," do you start to yawn? Do you see Scripture as a set of rules to obey? A list of propositions to believe? A series of stories to learn?

Ugh!

If that's what we think, we have missed it. We have failed to realize that at its very heart the Bible tells God's story. It is the epic narrative of the Creator creating this world…of the world failing to become what he intended because of human sin and evil…and of God redeeming it all and eventually making it exactly as he envisioned. God has a story. It's a tale that stretches from creation to re-creation, from Genesis to Revelation, from beginning to end…and even on to a new beginning that will *never* end.

In one sentence, God's story as revealed in the Bible is this: God created a world of humans whom he could know and love, and despite their stubbornness and rebellion, reconciled them to himself through his own sacrificial love. All the other stories in the Bible find their fulfillment in that Great Story.

GOD'S STORY HAS EIGHT CHAPTERS

The Bible is filled with hundreds of stories. You can read about Adam and Eve, Abraham and Sarah, Moses and Joshua, David and Goliath, Elijah and Elisha, Ruth and Esther. And that's just the Old Testament! In the New Testament we encounter Mary and Joseph, Jesus and the Twelve, Peter and John, Herod and Pilate, Paul and Barnabas, and the list goes on.

While all are important, we have chosen to retell God's story in eight chapters. We have selected what we believe are the primary historical movements in the biblical story. The eight chapters correspond to these movements. Each chapter also focuses on a strategic character whom God uses to advance his Story. Taken together, these eight chapters tell God's Great Story. The overall story arc goes like this:

- God creates (Adam and Eve)

- God blesses (Abraham)

- God rescues (Moses)

- God chooses (David)

- God warns (Hosea)

- God saves (Jesus)

- God sends (Paul)

- God wins (John)

GOD'S STORY HAS A LOT
OF LITTLE STORIES AS WELL

Between the eight big stories, you will find hundreds of little stories. Some are important to the overall plotline; others, not as much. But if you are not at least familiar with their basic contours, the Big Story can seem disjointed.

So between chapters you will find what we are calling "The Story Between the Story." These seven summaries will take you on a whimsical tour of the many narratives we can't tell. They highlight the people and events that will fill in the gaps of your knowledge. The style is different from chapters 1 through 8. It's more playful and lighthearted—even snarky at times. And it's that way for two reasons: First, we want the overall story arc to be complete, even if the minor narratives are merely summarized. And second, we want you to enjoy learning what otherwise could qualify as Bible trivia. A spoonful of sugar still helps the medicine go down.

GOD'S STORY MAKES SENSE OF YOUR STORY

You probably know what it's like to lie in bed at night and ask, "Why is my life turning out like it is? Why has my story taken all these twists and turns?" You may be thinking about today's bloopers, yesterday's blow-ups, or last year's blunders. Wherever your mind goes, you want to make sense of it all.

If you're not making much progress, it may be that you're focusing only on your own life. Why not expand your vision and look at your story in light of God's story?

Seeing your life in light of God's story is the only way to make sense of your story.

So have a seat and listen up. God is about to tell you his Great Story.

1

GOD CREATES

Before there is space or time or anything else that we categorize as part of our world, there is God. Majestic and mysterious. All in all. Nothing and nobody else.

In infinite wisdom, and out of eternal love, God decides to create a world of beauty and order. He also decides to create humans to live in that world. He will make them like himself, able to think, feel, will, relate, and create. This means that they will be free, able to choose, capable of saying yes or no to their Creator.

So he starts creating.

And the results are breathtaking. At the mention of a mere word, galaxies whirl into place, oceans fill the deep spaces, and living creatures appear to rule them all. God takes a special interest in humans, endowing them with gifts and abilities to oversee his whole creation. This is the story of creation in a nutshell.

CREATION AND GENESIS 1

When you hear "God creates," what do you picture?

Do you picture the glories of the universe?

- The amazing auroras of the Northern Lights?

- The sun-drenched beaches of Hawaii and Barbados?

- The rugged grandeur of the Grand Canyon and the Grand Tetons?

Or do you picture the nasty arguments that have plagued the church?

- The Copernican Revolution, in which Copernicus and Galileo challenged church teaching with their claim that the earth revolved around the sun, not vice versa?

- The Scopes Monkey Trial, where defense attorney Clarence Darrow portrayed Christians as dunces for believing in creation?

- Science textbook debates, which have politicized the issue by asking whether science is an enemy of faith or its friend?

Thankfully, the creation-science conversation is friendlier now than at any time in recent memory. Productive discussions are taking place. But as important as that is, we have a different focus. We want to tell God's Great Story. And the first chapter is all about creation.

So in a spirit of discovery and humility, we invite you to open your Bible to the opening chapters in Genesis. As you do so, remember that *how* you read

Genesis 1 is as important as *what* you read there. Here's how we suggest you read these iconic chapters.

HOW TO READ GENESIS 1

Genesis 1 Is Prehistoric

When you read the word "prehistoric," don't picture a triceratops fighting a tyrannosaurus rex, or a snaggletoothed caveman defending himself against both. "Prehistoric" means that these events occurred before history was recorded. The earliest Bible event that we can date with any accuracy is the call of Abraham, which occurred around 2000 BC.[1] Genesis 1 describes ancient events that not only predate Abraham but also point to the earliest moments of cosmic history. That means nobody was there from Eyewitness News to get the story. No human observed the act of creation, writing it all down for posterity.

We believe that God created the heavens and the earth. We also believe that someone under God's guidance wrote about it at a later point. But we don't know how much later. What we do know is that the creation story describes events that occurred before people wrote down history. That's what prehistoric means.

Genesis 1 Is Prescientific

The ancient Hebrews had no knowledge of the Copernican revolution—they had no idea that the earth revolves around the sun. Yet God was pleased to reveal himself to people who never dreamed that the sun was the center of the universe. When he inspired them to write Genesis 1, God did not whisper, "Pssst, since you are writing this down for posterity, be sure to give a heliocentric worldview.

It won't make sense to you now, but it will to future readers." It's laughable when you think about it that way. Genesis 1 is geocentric, and that is apparently fine with God. If you're a science-lover, don't let this bother you—any more than it should bother you that David described his own intrauterine development without benefiting from the modern science of embryology. Yet I wouldn't want to remove these words from the Bible:

> You created my inmost being;
>> you knit me together in my mother's womb.
> I praise you because I am fearfully and wonderfully made;
>> your works are wonderful,
>> I know that full well.
> My frame was not hidden from you
>> when I was made in the secret place,
>> when I was woven together in the depths of the earth.
> Your eyes saw my unformed body;
>> all the days ordained for me were written in your book
>> before one of them came to be.[2]

Would you?

While David was scientifically naive, he was theologically right on target. Don't get your science from the Bible any more than you get your theology from science.

Genesis 1 Is Theological

"Theology" is a rich word that comes from two Greek words: *theos*, which means "God," and *logos*, which means "study." Genesis 1 is primarily a study of God. These chapters tell of a God who created a wonderful world in which he placed intelligent humans and designed them to thrive. It's the story of a world where people are designed to enjoy a close connection with God, with one another, and with all of creation. To say it more simply, Genesis 1 is not about *how* and *when* the world was created, but about *Who* created it and *why*. If you focus on the *how* and *when*, you will treat those who disagree with you as enemies...or you will regard science as the enemy. And you will miss what God is trying to say to you about himself. But if you look for the *Who* and the *why*, then this deeply theological passage will yield rich insights.

So let's dive in.

THE MAIN CHARACTER IS GOD

"In the beginning God created the heavens and the earth."[3]

While you will meet many characters in Genesis, the creation story is all about the Creator.

GOD CREATED EVERYTHING

The chronology that the author uses is seven days. In Hebrew, the word "day" is *yom*. Your calendar may alert you to the annual celebration of the Jewish holy day called *Yom Kippur*, the Day of Atonement. *Yom* can mean a literal day, and in the Bible, it often means just that. But it doesn't have to mean a twenty-four-hour period of time. It can also refer to an unspecified period in the future. This is what it means when the prophets tell Israel to beware of "the day of the Lord," when he will judge his people. They weren't promising that God would execute his judgment within the parameters of twenty-four hours, but that however long it took, God would eventually implement his verdict. When we read how the story of Israel tragically ends,[4] this is exactly what we find. "The day of the Lord" took several decades, sometimes even centuries, to occur.

We believe that when "day" is used in Genesis 1–2, it points to an indefinite period of time, not to twenty-four literal hours. It refers to however long it took for God to create the heavens and the earth. But it's okay if you think differently on that issue. What matters is that we agree on what's most important: God created it all. Whether he did so instantaneously or gradually, whether "day" means literally twenty-four hours or figuratively points to a long period of time, God is still the Creator.[5]

Now let's look at each of the "days" of creation.

Days one, two, and three point to the three spheres of reality that God has created. These spheres describe the limits and boundaries in which we live: time, space, and earth.

Day One: Time

> Then God said, "Let there be light," and there was light. And God saw that the light was good. Then he separated the light from the darkness. God called the light "day" and the darkness "night." And evening passed and morning came, marking the first day.[6]

Before God created this world, time as we know it didn't exist. Father, Son, and Spirit interacted with one another throughout eternity—timelessly, effortlessly, joyfully. But with the introduction of day and night, time came into existence. Time refers to the progression of events as we experience them, from future (unknown) to present (now) to past (memory). While we mark time at a macrolevel (centuries) or at a microlevel (seconds), mostly we mark time in terms of days. We ask ourselves, "I wonder what today will hold for me?" We pray, "Give us today our daily bread." We say, "One day at a time." Day one is all about time.

Day Two: Space

> Then God said, "Let there be a space between the waters, to separate the waters of the heavens from the waters of the earth." And that is what happened. God made this space to separate the waters of the earth from the waters of the heavens. God called the space "sky." And evening passed and morning came, marking the second day.[7]

The dimension of space refers to the open skies immediately over us, outer space way above us, and "deep space" astronomically beyond us.

Day Three: The Earth

> Then God said, "Let the waters beneath the sky flow together into one place, so dry ground may appear." And that is what happened. God called the dry ground "land" and the waters "seas." And God saw that it was good. Then God said, "Let the land sprout with vegetation—every sort of seed-bearing plant, and trees that grow seed-bearing fruit. These seeds will then produce the kinds of plants and trees from which they came."

And that is what happened. The land produced vegetation—all sorts of seed-bearing plants, and trees with seed-bearing fruit. Their seeds produced plants and trees of the same kind. And God saw that it was good. And evening passed and morning came, marking the third day.[8]

Earth includes land, along with all the God-ordained gifts and processes we call vegetation, which become the basis for human sustenance. Plants, trees, and fruits are given to nourish us. So in the three "days" of creation found in Genesis 1, we see God creating time, space, and the earth.

Days Four, Five, and Six

When we come to days four, five, and six, we see that the events are carefully orchestrated. Each day points to an assigned ruler over the spheres named in the first three days.

Day four identifies the sun and the moon as God's creation. What would their role be? The sun would rule the day; the moon would rule the night.[9] Day five corresponds to day two. What's created on day five? Birds and fish—birds to fill the open space above us, and fish to fill the deep watery space below us. The birds rule the air, the fish rule the sea.[10] On day six, God creates animals and humans, referring back to day three. What did God do on day three? He created the earth. And the humans and animals on day six are called to rule it.[11]

GOD RESTED

The story ends with day seven. That's when God rested.

So the creation of the heavens and the earth and everything
in them was completed. On the seventh day God had finished
his work of creation, so he rested from all his work. And God
blessed the seventh day and declared it holy, because it was
the day when he rested from all his work of creation.[12]

If you think the phrase "God rested" meant God was exhausted after spending six days making galaxies and gorillas and geckos, you're not alone. Many of us picture God as being so worn out that he needed a divine nap. If so, we've missed the point.

Day seven does not depict the rest of exhaustion—it points to the rest of celebration. Everything is in its right place. Everything is in order. Everything is functioning just like God intended. This is what *shalom* means. And this is what God celebrated when he looked at all he had done.

GOD CREATED HUMANS

We skipped over something on day six that is pretty important. Let's go back.

Then God said, "Let us make human beings in our image, to
be like us. They will reign over the fish in the sea, the birds in
the sky, the livestock, all the wild animals on the earth, and the
small animals that scurry along the ground."

So God created human beings in his own image.
In the image of God he created them;
male and female he created them.

> Then God blessed them and said, "Be fruitful and multiply.
> Fill the earth and govern it. Reign over the fish in the sea,
> the birds in the sky, and all the animals that scurry along
> the ground."[13]

The apex of all creation is humans who are made in the image of God. You could hardly find a more revolutionary teaching: mortal, finite humans are created to be like the immortal, infinite Creator! This doesn't suggest that no other creatures bring glory to God—no doubt all do. Although in my humble opinion, gnats and mosquitoes are questionable…as are rats and snakes. But according to Genesis, we know that humans, of all God's creation, are made like God.

Being created in the image of God means that our mind, emotions, and will reflect the thinking, feeling, and willing of God. More than anything, it means we are made to relate like God relates to us. God is relational, so he has put the same capacity and drive into each of us. We are designed to connect meaningfully to God and to others. We are also made to govern the world on God's behalf, to represent him on the earth as corulers, cocreators.

But God sees that something isn't quite right. So he addresses it head-on.

GOD CREATED MARRIAGE

> Then the Lord God said, "It is not good for the man to be alone.
> I will make a helper who is just right for him…"
> So the Lord God caused the man to fall into a deep sleep.
> While the man slept, the Lord God took out one of the man's
> ribs and closed up the opening. Then the Lord God made a
> woman from the rib, and he brought her to the man.

"At last!" the man exclaimed. "This one is bone from my bone, and flesh from my flesh! She will be called 'woman,' because she was taken from 'man.'"

This explains why a man leaves his father and mother and is joined to his wife, and the two are united into one.[14]

When God looks at the man, he exclaims, "Wait a minute! You still look lonely to me!" God's answer to human loneliness is marriage. With all its promise and pitfalls, marriage is a gift from God. That doesn't mean you are inadequate if you are unmarried. (I'd hate to tell Jesus that his life was incomplete because he never married.) But for most humans, marriage is the norm. It is God's designated answer to loneliness.

A Deeper Look at Marriage

As we look deeper into Genesis 2:22-24, we see four things about God's original intent for marriage. First, marriage was to be binary: between a man and a woman. Second, it was to be exclusive. The man leaves his parents and is joined to the woman. He does not stay with her for a while, then leave and join himself to another woman, then repeat that pattern as often as he wishes. Third, marriage is to be permanent, which is the meaning behind "the two are united into one." Finally, it is a relationship of equality. Both are made in the image of God, with equal access to God. The best marriages are characterized by mutuality, partnership, and deep respect.

WHAT CREATION MEANS TO US

When you reflect on God as Creator, you will likely be inspired and moved.

Creation Is a Gift

God did not have to make the world. He didn't have to make you. Creation wasn't necessary as if God were incomplete and needed something to fulfill him.

God created simply because he wanted to. Why? Because God is love. It's that simple. Before the world came into being, God existed as three-in-one Majesty. Living in a circle of perfect love, Father, Son, and Spirit freely related to each other, joyfully reveled in each other, and humbly submitted to one another. There was never a time when the Father did not love the Son and the Spirit, or when the Son did not love the Father and the Spirit, or when the Spirit did not love the Father and the Son. In that circle of threefold unity, God was so filled with love that he decided to create humans in order to have someone else to love. That's a gift, pure and simple.

Creation Is Good

In Genesis 1 the word "good" is used six times to describe creation, and "very good" is used once. What God made was originally wonderful. We know from experience that sin and evil have defaced it and made it ugly. But that does not diminish the beauty of the original creation. (You'll have to wait for chapter 8 to see how God finally redeems what we humans have messed up!)

Creation Is Purposeful

God's meta-purpose is not stated in Genesis 1–2, but it's clear in the New Testament: creation is through and for Jesus. Although the name *Jesus* is not found in Genesis 1–2, we can imagine God saying to his beloved Son before all creation, "Son, I want us to build something together. It's going to be spectacular! And when we finish building it, I want to give it to you as a gift." As the apostle Paul writes in the New Testament:

Christ is the visible image of the invisible God.

He existed before anything was created and is supreme
over all creation,

for through him God created everything
in the heavenly realms and on earth.

He made the things we can see
and the things we can't see—

such as thrones, kingdoms, rulers, and authorities in the
unseen world.

Everything was created through him and for him.[15]

THE REST OF THE STORY

The Story Goes South

Creation is chapter 1 in God's Great Story. It's a picture of beauty, power, and grandeur—the stuff of dreams come true. But soon the dreams turn into nightmares. The story goes south.

What happens? Adam and Eve decide that they want to be like God. They want to know all that their Maker knows. They want to create their own lives, without reference to the One who created them. Simply put, they rebel.

The results are dreadful. Sin enters the world. Our enemy secures a foothold. The image of God in humans is disfigured. Married couples struggle. Siblings kill each other. Nations go to war. Eden seems lost.

But that's not the end of the story.

God Doesn't Give Up

Despite the rebellion of the human race, God doesn't give up on his fallen creatures. We are still the apple of his eye. He is determined to fulfill his purposes for creation, whatever it takes. The rest of God's Story shows the extent to which he is committed to that vision.

It's one thing to say you *believe* in God's Story. It's an altogether different thing to say you *belong* in God's Story. But you do. All of us do. As Genesis 1 winds up, we discover our job description as humans in God's creation.

> Then God blessed them and said, "Be fruitful and multiply. Fill the earth and govern it. Reign over the fish in the sea, the birds in the sky, and all the animals that scurry along the ground."[16]

We are to govern and rule over God's creation. Here's what that means.

You Are God's Apprentice

While God is senior Creator, he has chosen to make you one of his junior creators—a business partner, if you will. He wants you to use your intellect and imagination to create human culture. Utilizing your energy and ingenuity, he invites you to create (and constantly improve) the building-blocks of society: agriculture and commerce, art and music, technology and science, politics and education, family life and leisure. The scope of God's vision for your creativity is breathtaking. He wants you to help make the world more like he intended it to be. You are his apprentice.

You Are God's Manager

While God owns all he has made, he has entrusted you with its management. This raises the topic of how we treat the heavens and the earth. Sadly, the environmental debate has degenerated into a shouting match—lots of heat but little light. Whatever your thoughts on the topic, however, one thing is abundantly clear: Christians should lead the way in promoting and living out wise and healthy ways of caring for God's good creation. We must pass on a habitable world to the next generation.

You Are God's Representative

A representative is someone who officially mirrors the vision of one nation to another nation. That means God has appointed you to embody him in the world. He has placed you on earth to mirror to others who he really is and to love those whom he deeply loves. Here's what being a representative might look like in your circles of influence.

Representatives at Home

A mom in our church was worried about her teenage daughter and some questionable decisions she was making. The mom didn't want to come on too strong with the Bible, so she asked if they could read a devotional together each night. The daughter said yes. As a result, they had many deep, personal conversations about faith and life. This mother was gently mirroring God's love to her daughter. She was faithfully fulfilling the role of God's representative.

Representatives at Work

We have a friend who has the rare combination of high IQ and high EQ. He could make a good salary in the private sector if he wanted to. Instead, he chooses to work in a governmental agency. His job is thankless. Few people show gratitude, and many are demanding and hostile. Yet he remains in this job so he can serve people and show them the character of Christ. He feels like God has called him to the public sector so he can reflect God's character to a watching world. He is God's representative in a federal workplace.

Representatives in Your Neighborhood

We know a handyman who can fix anything. (And we should know—we can't fix much of anything.) But one of his greatest gifts is the way he serves his neighbors. While he lives alone with his Rottweilers, he sees all his neighbors as family. He invites them over for burgers and steaks, does free repairs on their homes, and provides them with a sense of community and connection. He is God's representative in his neighborhood.

Representatives in Your World

When the world shows you ugliness and hatred, reflecting God's love seems impossible. But some have found a way to mirror God's love to their enemies. In the summer of 2015, several families in Charleston, South Carolina, lost loved ones when a deranged killer opened fire on parishioners on a Wednesday night at Emanuel African Methodist Episcopal Church. When some of the survivors spoke to the assassin two days later at his court appearance through videoconferencing, what they said stunned the world:

"I forgive you," said the tearful daughter of victim Ethel Lance,
70. "You took something very precious from me and I will never
talk to [my mother] ever again. I will never be able to hold her
again. But I forgive you. And have mercy on your soul."

"I forgive you," said Anthony Thompson, the husband of slain
wife Myra, 59. "But we would like you to take this opportunity
to repent. Repent, confess, give your life to the one who
matters most: Christ. So that he can change it, can change
your ways no matter what happened to you and you'll be okay.
Do that, and you'll be better off than what you are right now."[17]

In his grace, the Creator has written you into his story of creation. You have an important role to play as apprentice, manager, and representative. Don't underestimate the significance of being a human creature in the Creator's world.

JUST THE BEGINNING

God's creation of the world is just the beginning of his Great Story. What's next? In the following chapters we encounter a God who...

- blesses the world by beginning a new nation through an old Bedouin shepherd and his wife,

- rescues his people from slavery and delivers them to the Land of Promise,

- chooses a young man "after God's heart" to lead his people,

- warns his people through prophets that they must straighten up if they are to be his people,

- saves the world through a Jewish carpenter who is also the Son of God,

- sends the Good News out into the world through a rabbi-turned-apostle, and

- wins the final victory over sin, evil, and death by ushering in a new heavens and new earth.

Buckle your seatbelts!

THE STORY BETWEEN THE STORY

After Adam and Eve are banished from the Garden, they have Cain and Abel. The first recorded case of sibling rivalry happens when God accepts Abel's offering but rejects Cain's. It gets intense. Cain kills Abel, is banished from his family, settles east of Eden, marries, has a son he names Enoch and founds a city he names…Enoch. Apparently, while Cain was a great farmer, he was not a creative thinker.

As more and more people fill the earth, mankind becomes increasingly wicked. God is sorry he ever created humans, and his heart is broken. In all the earth, only Noah is righteous, so God instructs him to build a huge boat to save the animals and his family from a catastrophic flood. After the waters recede and they're again on dry land, Noah builds an altar to offer sacrifices to God, and God gives a rainbow as a sign of his covenant to never again destroy all living things.

God blesses Noah and his sons Shem, Ham, and Japheth, commanding them to be fruitful and multiply, which seems to be the one commandment humans can obey. Soon the earth is populous, everyone speaks the same language, and they think they're the coolest thing since sliced bread (which has not yet been invented). With the goal of displaying their general awesomeness to the world, the people build a great city with a tower reaching to the sky. God says, "Yeah, no," and confuses their language so they stop building and scatter.

One of Noah's sons, Shem, has a particularly important lineage: Shem has Arphaxad, who has Shelah, who has Eber, who has Peleg, who has Reu, who has Serug, who has Nahor, who has Terah, who has Abram, who lived in the land of Ur.

Abram marries a woman named Sarai. His father Terah takes Abram, Sarai, and Abram's nephew, Lot, and heads from Ur toward Canaan. But they stop and settle in Haran.

And that, in a nutshell, is the story between the story.

HARAN

CANAAN

UR

Abram

Sarai

Isaac

Cain

2nd

Abel

1st

GOD BLESSES

Several years into the family adventure in Haran, the Lord comes to Abram, now seventy-five and looking toward retirement. Much to his surprise, God makes him an offer he'd be crazy to refuse—picturesque land, thousands of descendants, way more than fifteen minutes of fame, and a generational legacy. There's just one catch. He will have to give up most everything near and dear to him—his country home, his father's family, and lifetime friends. Throwing caution to the wind, Abram packs ups his belongings, says his goodbyes, and is off on a new adventure.

The linchpin of this whole enterprise is the birth of a son who can begin a new family line. The trouble is, Sarai never conceived when her biological clock was ticking, and by now it has been years since Sarai had her last hot flash. Call them crazy, but Abram and Sarai trusted that God would make a way for his promise to be fulfilled. They just had no idea it would take him another twenty-five years to get the job done.

In the meantime, God decides to give Abram and Sarai new names—Abraham and Sarah—which puzzles Abraham at first. "Sarai" in Hebrew means "whiny and quarrelsome;" "Sarah" means "princess." You can see Abraham's dilemma: Would he prefer being married to a whiny complainer or a high-maintenance princess? Thankfully, Sarah is a princess in the very best sense of the word, and Abraham loves her dearly.

The time finally arrives, and the Lord shows up with a small entourage of angels. Sarah, now ninety, overhears their conversation and bursts out laughing. After an awkward pause, the Lord decides Abraham and Sarah should name the baby Isaac, which means "laughter."

So when Abraham turns 100, Isaac is born, and the cornerstone of God's promise is laid. Isaac will have two sons—Jacob and Esau—and Jacob will have twelve sons who become the twelve tribes of Israel. And that is Abraham's story in a nutshell.[1]

GOD'S STORY

God's Story is not a monologue. Being other-centered in his essential nature, he invites other characters onto the stage to help carry the dialogue, move the action along, and reveal his gracious nature and purpose for creation. God's interaction with Abraham continues the grand unveiling of who God is, who we are, what he is up to, and why we are here. To get to the heart of these matters, let's explore God's role in this chapter of his Great Story.

The reason Abraham's story is so significant is that God reboots his relationship with human beings when he reaches out and invites Abraham to become a full partner with him in his earthly enterprise. God and Abraham seal the deal by making a covenant with each other. A covenant is an agreement between two parties that lays out the benefits and responsibilities of each party. While this may sound more like a contract, there is a crucial distinction. Rabbi Jonathan Sacks points out the difference, "A contract is a *transaction*. A covenant is a *relationship*. Or to put it slightly differently: a contract is about interests. A covenant is about identity. It is about you and me coming together to form an 'us.' That is why contracts *benefit*, but covenants *transform*."[2] This new covenant transforms Abraham's life and ultimately provides the relational foundation and context for the rest of God's Great Story.

While the details of God's and Abraham's relationship take thirteen chapters of Genesis to cover, it's the invitation to the covenant that reveals the hope and heart of God. Here's how Genesis records it:

> The LORD had said to Abram, "Leave your native country, your relatives, and your father's family, and go to the land that I will show you. I will make you into a great nation. I will bless you and make you famous, and you will be a blessing to others. I will bless those who bless you and curse those who treat you with contempt. All the families on earth will be blessed through you."[3]

These three short verses are the genesis of the story arc of God's redeeming work in and through the nation of Israel. Not surprisingly then, out of the establishment of this covenant the seminal plotlines of God's Great Story will flow. Some if not all of these plotlines will be evident in every chapter of God's Great Story. They are the recurring threads that hold the Story together and ultimately create the profoundly beautiful tapestry of mankind's living history with God. Here they are…

GOD'S PURPOSE

I think it's safe to say God doesn't do things by accident. He always does things on purpose. Reaching out to Abraham was God's intentional effort to create a community of people he could love and call his own. For a God whose essential nature is "loving relationship"—think Father, Son, and Holy Spirit—having a deeply meaningful relationship with his creation naturally follows. That's why throughout the Old and New Testaments you find statements like "You will be my people and I will be your God." Some form of this sentiment occurs fifty-one times in the Bible. The first is in Genesis 17:7, when God speaks to Abraham, and the last is in Revelation 21:3, where at the end of time John envisions God making all things new and declares, "God's home is now among his people! He will live with them, and they will be his people. God himself will be with them."

This purpose is the underlying motivation for God's call to Abraham. He's inviting him to become the progenitor of this new community of people who will live in life-giving fellowship with God. And it's not meant to be a small, cozy, inward-facing family. It's to be a God-sized community that eventually incorporates all peoples, nations, and ethnicities into one big family. As you continue to read God's Great Story, you will notice this purpose is the through-line in the succeeding chapters.

GOD'S POSTURE

If God is seeking to create a people to love and call his own, it makes total sense that he would give them his favor and blessing. As our story opens, we find the words "bless" or "blessing" used five times in just two verses as God lays out his proposition to Abraham.[4] Even a cursory reading reveals there is a whole lot of blessing going on in God's Great Story—over 600 mentions in the Old Testament alone. Something that pops up that many times is worth a closer look. When God blesses mankind in creation, it means that he embeds within the normal flow and mystery of existence a generative power for life, fertility, and well-being.[5] When he blesses an individual, like Abraham, it means that he declares his favor and vested interest in seeing that person experience life and prosperity. In Abraham's case, God gets down to brass tacks pretty quickly. Land, descendants, and prominence are all on the offer sheet. We are barely beyond the prologue of God's Great Story, and it is already becoming clear that God is downright serious about blessing people.

He's so serious in fact, that in the small print of Abraham's agreement God asserts that he is not just going to bless Abraham through this new arrangement, but he's also going to work a side deal through Abraham to bless *all* the families on earth! This side hustle inspires one of the better adages to come out of God's Great Story—"We are blessed to be a blessing."

Keep an eye out for that last sentiment because it shows up frequently, especially when we get to the New Testament chapters in God's Great Story. You'll hear Jesus say things like, "Freely you have received, freely give." "As I have loved you, so you must love one another." You'll hear Paul, one of the first spiritual leaders in Jesus's new movement, say, "[Forgive] each other, just as in Christ God forgave you."[6] God is so intent on multiplying his blessing to all families everywhere that he writes a "pay it forward" clause into every new relationship agreement he strikes.

GOD'S INVITATION

You can learn a lot about someone by observing how they enter into and carry on relationships. One could surmise that God had numerous options available as he sought to re-create a community of people to call his own. After two false starts, first with Adam and Eve and then with Noah's neighbors, who would blame God if he just decided to install some new software in the human brain so everyone would automatically think, say, and do exactly what he wanted? No muss, no fuss. He could have simply made us robots. But it would take God about a nanosecond to figure out there would be no relational satisfaction in such a scenario.

Or, in the spirit of *The Godfather*, God could have made Abraham "an offer he couldn't refuse" implying, of course, that if Abraham didn't bite, one day he might wake up to a severed yak head in his bed. Once again, what kind of relational joy would God find in throwing a party where people only came because they were threatened with mortal harm if they didn't?

To the contrary, God understands that true love flourishes only where each party has the freedom to love, or not. That's why his bid for a relationship with humans always comes in the form of an invitation. No threat. No coercion. No arm twisting. Just a gracious offer. Most often, though, as with Abraham, God's invitations involve high risk and high reward.

GOD'S DESIRED RESPONSE

With every invitation offered, an RSVP is implied. Certainly this is the case for Abraham. Things can get lost in translation, but the writer of Genesis doesn't leave much doubt. At God's invitation, Abraham packs up his tents, toys, and essential personnel, beginning with his wife and favorite nephew, and heads off to his new home. Here is how Genesis records it:

> So Abram departed as the Lord had instructed, and Lot went with him. Abram was seventy-five years old when he left Haran. He took his wife, Sarai, his nephew Lot, and all his wealth—his livestock and all the people he had taken into his household at Haran—and headed for the land of Canaan. When they arrived in Canaan, Abram traveled through the land as far as Shechem. There he set up camp beside the oak of Moreh. At that time, the area was inhabited by Canaanites. Then the Lord appeared to Abram and said, "I will give this land to your descendants." And Abram built an altar there and dedicated it to the Lord, who had appeared to him.[7]

Abraham's reaction is the quintessential picture of trust. Note that we use the word "trust" instead of "faith" in the description of this plotline. Both are good words and accurate translations of their Hebrew and Greek roots. However, time has done a funky thing to the etymology of these two English words, and "trust" captures Abraham's response most accurately. Here's why. The word "faith" in English is used as a noun only. "Trust" in English is a noun *and* a verb. What Abraham did in response to God's promise has a distinctly verbal quality to it. He doesn't just trust that God *can* fulfill the promise, he trusts that he *will*, and so he packs up the U-Haul and heads west.

The response that God looks for is never a noun only. It is always a noun plus a verb. Abraham had a belief (noun) about God's trustworthiness and power, and he was willing to reorder (verb) his whole life around what he now believed to be true. This is such an iconic response that near the end of God's Great Story, two New Testament writers hold Abraham up as a shining example and hero of faith![8]

Abraham's trust in the promise does not go unrewarded. God comes through on all the stipulations of his original offer. Abraham indeed becomes one of the most influential individuals in history. The three largest monotheistic religions—Judaism, Christianity, and Islam—trace their origins to him. This man, who was approaching the century mark childless, now has four billion people who call him "father Abraham." Which brings us to the last plotline.

GOD'S CHARACTER IS DEMONSTRATED

Although God is rarely on Abraham's timetable, he fulfills his promise in spades. Despite Abraham's and Sarah's impatience, scheming, and doubting, God's faithfulness is a tangible demonstration of the nature of his character. Genesis declares:

> The LORD kept his word and did for Sarah exactly what he had promised. She became pregnant, and she gave birth to a son for Abraham in his old age. This happened at just the time God had said it would. And Abraham named their son Isaac. Eight days after Isaac was born, Abraham circumcised him as God had commanded. Abraham was 100 years old when Isaac was born. And Sarah declared, "God has brought me laughter. All who hear about this will laugh with me. Who would have said to Abraham that Sarah would nurse a baby? Yet I have given Abraham a son in his old age!"[9]

As God's Great Story reveals, the promise to Abraham becomes the touchstone for his descendants, the people of Israel. Whenever they are threatened, bloodied, or beaten, it is this promise they cling to for dear life. The arc of God's story is long, and his people discover that his faithfulness is not a limited resource. Through every generation, he makes his faithfulness known by rescuing, renewing, forgiving, and restoring his people again and again. And here's more good news: you are included in the story too!

We love stories because something in us readily identifies with particular characters, and they draw us in vicariously. One of the aspects of Abraham's and Sarah's story that we have not yet explored might be the point at which you resonate most with God's Great Story. It has to do with the presence of barrenness in their lives.

THE CURSE OF BARRENNESS

Sarah was infertile and everybody knew it. Back in the day, being childless carried with it all kinds of negative implications. Barrenness was considered a disability, a stigma. It easily became the defining characteristic of a woman, bringing a sense of shame and debilitating hopelessness.

It wasn't much better for Abraham. Sarah's barrenness meant no heirs and the end of the line for his branch on the family tree. Barrenness was the cloud hanging over them and following them wherever they went. Life was slipping away, and understandably, any hope of a different ending had died with Sarah's last hot flash.

Abraham's barrenness also had a spiritual component. He had grown up in a family that worshipped many gods. Some were territorial or neighborhood gods. Others were ancestral gods tied to family members from days gone by. Still others were functional in nature: gods of fertility, healing, the weather, you name it. What was perhaps most frustrating for Abraham is that these gods were impersonal. They didn't care much for people. In fact, if you didn't keep them happy, they would punish you. As a result, people felt compelled to offer sacrifices in order to keep the gods happy and ensure themselves a better crop, a fertile womb, and plenty of protection.

The trouble with this arrangement is that it caused a lot of anxiety. How could a person ever know if they had sacrificed enough to make the gods happy? Were two pigeons enough? If not, next year sacrifice a lamb or a calf? Still not getting the results you want? Sacrifice more! You see where this is going. This tension drove people to keep upping the sacrificial ante…some even to the point of sacrificing their own children. To top it off, the whole process was terribly soulless. It was just a transaction. It was the cost of doing business. Having a personal relationship with any of the gods could not have been further from anyone's mind.

GOD SPEAKS HOPE

It is into this barrenness of body and soul that God speaks a word of hope to Abraham, who is more than primed to listen. Perhaps like Abraham and Sarah, you have experienced barrenness in body or soul. Barrenness is a powerful metaphor that communicates across time and cultures. The unfulfilled desire to bring a new life into the world has caused more hearts to break and tears to fall than can be counted. Marriages have broken, hopes have been crushed, and faith has been tested when this deep human yearning has gone unmet.

Barrenness can also describe our basic frame of reference. There are times when we look at life and see only sepia tones. The landscape is dry and dirty. There is no buzz of energy, no forward motion, no real life to speak of. Call it sadness, or depression, or despair, but no matter how you slice it, it feels empty, cold, barren.

Barrenness can infect any segment of our lives. We can be spiritually, relationally, emotionally, vocationally, or even financially barren. Whenever and wherever we feel alone, unfulfilled, or tapped out, barrenness has moved into our neighborhood. Thankfully, God has included us in his promise to Abraham! Not to get too far ahead of ourselves, but toward the end of God's Great Story you'll learn more about the apostle Paul, who is mentioned earlier. On one occasion he writes an encouraging letter to a group of Jesus's followers living in the city of Galatia:

> In the same way, "Abraham believed God, and God counted him as righteous because of his faith." The real children of Abraham, then, are those who put their faith in God. What's more, the Scriptures looked forward to this time when God would declare the Gentiles to right in his sight because of their faith. God proclaimed this good news to Abraham long ago when he said, "All nations will be blessed through you." So all who put their faith in Christ share the same blessing Abraham received because of his faith.[10]

This is incredible news! In the same way that God reached out to Abraham, he is reaching out to you, offering you the promise of a blessed life. In Christ, God promises you a future radically different from your past. If you are living in the barrenness of addiction, loneliness, disappointment, or hopelessness, God can write a new chapter in your life. And all he requires from you is what he required of Abraham—trust!

We're early in the story, and there is still much to discover about God, his nature, and his plan to restore and reconcile all the families on earth back to himself. But as you learn more of his story, keep track of how often he is faithful to his promise in the lives of the people you're reading about. God's faithfulness does not have an expiration date. There is no limit to how many times he will show up and follow up on his promise to his people.

We know this firsthand. When we moved our families to Texas in 2002 to start a new church, it was in response to a calling and a promise. We left the comfort of large, established churches in the southeast to plant a church in north Texas with no people, no money, no building or land, and no sponsoring church. As you might imagine, starting a church from scratch is fraught with all kinds of challenges. Every step along the way, and on numerous occasions, God provided resources and people to help accomplish our vision.

At one particular juncture, we were running low on resources and urgently needed God to come through for us yet again. In our hearts we were starting to wonder just how often we could count on him to show up and demonstrate his faithfulness to us. There's got to be a limit, doesn't there, to the number of times you can "phone a heavenly friend" when planting a church? The answer came to us one afternoon while we were praying with some desperation. As we prayed, God's Spirit gave us these clarifying thoughts, "My last act of faithfulness was not my last act of faithfulness."

This simple phrase has become a life-giving axiom for us as we have continued to believe the promise God gave us. As you read more of God's Great Story, and as you think about your own, our prayer is that you will be able to say with great confidence that God has been astoundingly faithful to you too…and he's only getting started!

THE STORY BETWEEN THE STORY

When Abraham's son Isaac grows up, Abraham wants to find his son a wife. Enter Rebekah, who shows us that it always pays to water a man's camels. Turns out Rebekah is a relative of Isaac, but back then that's actually not a deal breaker—it's a bonus. Just go with it.

Isaac and Rebekah have twins—Esau and Jacob (think cats and dogs). Jacob steals Esau's birthright and blessing, skips town, and dreams of a stairway to heaven (minus guitar solo). He falls in love with his beautiful cousin Rachel (again, just go with it), but gets tricked into first marrying her sister Leah, who has a *great* personality. Jacob and Esau reconcile; Jacob wrestles with God (literally) and gets a new name: Israel. He has a whole bunch of kids but loves Rachel's son Joseph the best. Joseph is a dreamer and a bit of a smarty-pants, so his brothers decide to teach him a lesson by selling him into slavery and telling their father he's dead.

Joseph ends up in Egypt. God is with Joseph and he earns his Egyptian master's favor, but he's sent to prison for something he didn't do. After years in prison he interprets Pharaoh's crazy dream and goes from prison to the palace as Pharaoh's right-hand man. It all comes full circle when a famine forces Joseph's brothers to search for food in Egypt, and a dream Joseph had once told them about becomes a reality as they bow before the man they don't even recognize as their brother. Joseph forgives his brothers, is reunited with his father, and the whole family is invited to come and live like royalty in Egypt. This is how, for hundreds of years, the children of Israel come to live and prosper and multiply in the land of Egypt.

And that, in a nutshell, is the story between the story.

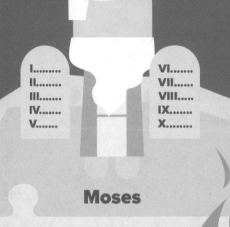

Moses

Israel

WELCOME TO THE
PROMISED LAND

GOD RESCUES

As you open the next chapter in God's Great Story, you might find yourself asking, "What the what?!" Instead of living in the lovely land of Canaan where God has promised they will settle down and have an awesome life, the Israelites are stuck in the dreaded land of Egypt. And it gets worse: they are slaves to the Egyptians, which is surely not a part of their deal with God. But as they are about to discover, when things look their worst, God is about to be at his best. When life feels like it's going down, expect God to show up.

Enter Moses, Israel's first and greatest spokesman for God. (He's quite a miracle-worker too.) Born into a common Jewish family, he is raised in a fancy Egyptian palace. Although trained for a life of leisure, he winds up in a desert for decades, counting sheep and bored out of his gourd. Certain that God has forgotten him, one day he has his sandals blown off when the God of his ancestors confronts him. Thinking he is heading into retirement at the age of eighty, he is given the, shall we say, "challenging" task of moving millions of Israelites out of Egypt and into the Land of Promise. Only God could pull off something that seemingly impossible!

Chapter 3 is the story of the exodus—not the Bible book, but the story that inspired the Bible book. It's the story of a God who shows up when he's least expected and powerfully rescues his people. It's the story of Moses. And, not coincidentally, it's your story.

God's story always involves choosing one person to lead many people. As we've just seen, God selects Abraham to start a new nation called Israel. Then God uses Abraham's kids and grandkids to multiply a small clan into a semi-nation. And when his people wind up in Egypt rather than in the Promised Land, God picks one person to get them back on track. Enter Moses.

GOD RESCUES MOSES

In every good story, someone gets in trouble and needs to be rescued. You will find this pattern throughout the Bible and therefore throughout this book. In chapter 3 of God's Great Story, the pattern goes like this: God rescues Moses, so that Moses can rescue Israel, so that Israel can rescue the world. Let's start with why God's people need rescuing.

Israel Suffers

God has already promised Abraham and his children's children that he will give them a home in Canaan. But a severe famine changes all that, and Jacob's family ends up moving to Egypt for food. When they arrive in Goshen, Abraham's great-grandson Joseph is the prime minister, so they have all the food they need. They live healthy lives and die at ripe, old ages.

Over the next 400 years, the Israelite population explodes. They are having kids left and right. And their children have children. And their children's children have children. *Ad infinitum.* Possibly *ad nauseam.* They clearly know the story of the birds and the bees.

They become so numerous that when a new Pharaoh comes to power who doesn't know Joe, he makes a big change. "We can't let these foreigners keep reproducing," he realizes. "They'll outnumber us, overpower us, and overthrow us. Let's make them our slaves!"

> So the Egyptians made the Israelites their slaves. They appointed brutal slave masters over them, hoping to wear them down with crushing labor...So the Egyptians worked the people of Israel without mercy. They made their lives bitter... They were ruthless in all their demands.[1]

But the Hebrews don't stop making babies. And Pharaoh won't change his mind. So he settles on a more violent solution: kill them. Not the adult slaves—that wouldn't make economic sense. Just kill the babies. Especially the boy babies. Drown them in the Nile River the minute they are born. Wow. Talk about a drastic measure for population control.[2]

Why Does God Let His People Suffer?

This story in Exodus is the first of many times you will read in the Bible that God's people, who are following him and his ways, are suffering. Why are they suffering? Are they doing something terrible that deserves divine judgment? Doesn't God care? Does he care but can't do anything about it?

The relation of God's silence to our suffering is one of the most perplexing questions you can ask. As Christian philosopher Peter Kreeft remarks, "There are many proofs or apparent proofs [that there is a God]…but there is only one argument that…claims to prove there is no God"—the argument that since evil exists, God must not.[3]

It is not wrong or faithless to wonder why we suffer. Especially when the God in whom we trust loves us dearly and is capable of saving us from all suffering. If you're looking for Bible support, just turn to the Psalms and start reading. You will find as many complaints as praises in those prayers. So complain to God all you want. He's not offended.

But we still need to consider the *why* question. The only answer that makes sense to us is that God has chosen to create us with the freedom to say yes or no to his plan. He could make us robots, but that would violate what it means to be made in his image—for God acts freely, not under compulsion. As all parents know, forced hugs from children don't mean much. We long for affection freely given. That brings us back to God's decision in creation: He could make us robots or free creatures. He has chosen the latter. But the freedom to say yes to God implies, even demands, the freedom to say no. And every time one of us says no to God and his plan, someone suffers. Think of bullying, crime, war. Or gluttony, adultery, prejudice. Or hatred, lying, #MeToo. Saying no to God always leads to suffering. This may not be an airtight answer, but it can help us live more faithfully in the midst of suffering.

God Intervenes

The Israelite slaves cry out, "God, where are you? You made this incredible promise to Abraham, but we don't see it being fulfilled. We're not in any Promised Land. We don't feel your blessing. We're not in the right place. And we're not sure that you even notice."

But God does notice. He is watching their plight and listening to their prayers. He decides to rescue them by sending a baby.

One day, a Hebrew woman gives birth to a little boy. We know him as Moses. But the parents defy Pharaoh's law and keep the boy alive. They can't hide him at home, because Egyptian soldiers are going house to house looking for Hebrew baby boys to kill. So the parents hatch an idea: "Let's put little Moses in a waterproof basket and hide him among the reeds on the bank of the Nile River. Soldiers won't look there. Maybe that will buy us some time. Or maybe God will show up and rescue our son. Wouldn't that be awesome!"

Awesome is just the right word for what happens next.

While Moses is floating along in the Nile, a daughter of Pharaoh notices the basket in the river and asks one of her servants to retrieve it. When she sees what is inside, she cries out, "Poor thing! He will die here in the river! I'll take him home with me and raise him in the palace." Then she realizes, "Uh-oh. I can bring him home, but I can't nurse him. How will he stay alive?" And as though following a divine cue, Moses's older sister, Miriam, steps out from the shadows of the riverbank where she has been watching the whole time. She tells the princess, "If you're looking for help, I happen to know someone who can raise this baby and nurse him until he's weaned." The princess has no better offers, so she accepts this one. And Miriam retrieves Moses's mother.

Do you see the hand of God at work? Moses is rescued, not drowned…his mother nurses him until he is weaned…and he is raised in safety in the royal court of Pharaoh. Only God.

"Only God"

What do you say when something happens that you can't explain? For instance,

- A complicated birth gives way to a healthy mother and infant.

- A family crisis finds resolution in a tearful reunion.

- A dead-end job morphs into a meaningful vocation.

You could say, "Wow! What a coincidence!" Or "I've never seen anything like that before!"

But as a follower of Christ, try saying, "Only God." As in, "Only God could turn something hopeless into something whole." That's what Moses's parents must have said when God rescued their little boy.

Moses Messes Up

Unexpectedly, the rescuer takes a detour. Although Moses gets the royal treatment as an adopted son of the Pharaoh, he gets bored living in the palace all the time. He has a hankering to see the real world—especially his Hebrew relatives. One day he ventures outside the palace and travels around the region. But instead of being impressed, he is horrified. He sees a form of injustice and brutality that would make any of us snap. And he does.

When Moses sees an Egyptian slave master beating an Israelite slave, he loses his cool. He kills the slave driver, buries him, looks around to make sure no one is watching, scurries back to the palace, and hopes nobody will find out. Uh-oh. The secret leaks. Everyone knows. Even the Pharaoh, who immediately puts a ransom on Moses's head.

What would you do? I know what I would do. I would run. That's what Moses does. He runs…across the Gulf of Suez, across the Gulf of Aqaba, until he reaches an area of Saudi Arabia called Midian. He isn't in a beautiful palace anymore. He is in an ugly desert. And the only way to survive in a desert is to find a flock of sheep and become a shepherd. So that's what he does. He also settles down, gets married, and starts a family. And being out in the desert day after day, he also thinks. All day, every day, for forty long years, Moses thinks. He's probably thinking about what a mess he's made of his life.

God Redeems Our Messes

Can God redeem our messes? If Moses is our model, then the answer is yes. God specializes in overcoming our mistakes. He seeks to lead us into "the paths of righteousness" (Psalm 23:2 KJV), but when we take the wrong route, he doesn't abandon us. He reaches back out in grace and mercy to guide us in the way he knows is best. And if we really mess things up? What then? Remember what Pastor Rick Warren says: "God never wastes a hurt."[4] It was true for Moses. It's true for you. God can turn your blunders into blessings.

God has now rescued Moses twice: after he is born, and after he commits murder. Both times, people are trying to kill him. Do you ever wonder why God keeps rescuing Moses?

GOD RESCUES MOSES TO RESCUE ISRAEL

God never rescues someone just for their sake. He always rescues them for the sake of others. In our highly individualistic society, that's not a self-evident truth. We value individuals so highly that it's easy to elevate their story over the story of the community in which they live. But in God's Kingdom, individuals are rescued so that they can be rescuers.

Moses Discovers God's Plan

Now it's time for God to tell Moses "The Plan"—God's plan for how he's going to persuade the Egyptians to release the Israelites so they can move to Canaan and build homes and families in the Promised Land. The plan initially is good news for Moses.

> One day Moses...led the flock far into the wilderness and came to Sinai, the Mountain of God. There the angel of the Lord appeared to him in a blazing fire from the middle of a bush. Moses stared in amazement. Though the bush was engulfed in flames, it didn't burn up. "This is amazing," Moses said to himself. "Why isn't that bush burning up? I must go see it."
>
> When the Lord saw Moses coming to take a closer look, God called to him from the middle of the bush, "Moses! Moses!"
>
> "Here I am!" Moses replied.

"Do not come any closer," the LORD warned. "Take off your sandals, for you are standing on holy ground. I am the God of your father—the God of Abraham, the God of Isaac, and the God of Jacob." When Moses heard this, he covered his face because he was afraid to look at God.

Then the LORD told him, "I have certainly seen the oppression of my people in Egypt. I have heard their cries of distress because of their harsh slave drivers. Yes, I am aware of their suffering. So I have come down to rescue them from the power of the Egyptians and lead them out of Egypt into their own fertile and spacious land."[5]

No doubt Moses cried out, "Praise God! He hasn't forgotten us! He has remembered his promise! He's finally going to rescue us!"

That's good news for Israel. But it's bad news for Moses.

"Now go, for I am sending you to Pharaoh."[6]

This is not on Moses's bucket list as he heads into his youthful eighties. He hasn't been thinking to himself, "Hey, why don't I go back to Egypt, where I'm wanted for murder? Why don't I look up ol' Pharaoh (who, last I heard, wants to kill me)? Why don't I tell him to release his free slave-labor? Maybe it'll be just like old times!"

Probably not.

So Moses begins to make excuses. First, he says, "God, why me? I have blood on my hands. I haven't seen Egypt for forty years. I wasn't raised with those Hebrews." But God answers, "I will be with you" (Exodus 3:12).

His second excuse is, "If the Israelites ask me, 'Who sent you?' what am I supposed to tell them? You have been silent for 400 years! They may not even remember you!" But God says, "You tell them, 'I am.' I am the God of Abraham, the God of Isaac, the God of Jacob. I am the promise-making God, I am the promise-keeping God, I am the rescuing God. I have not changed just because you haven't heard from me in four centuries. I. Am. Period."

Then Moses tries his third excuse. "What if they *still* won't believe me?" But God answers, "No biggie. I'll give you power to do miracles in their midst. That will get their attention."

But Moses is good at thinking up excuses. Maybe that's what happens if you tend sheep in the desert for decades. Which brings us to excuse number four: "I'm not a good speaker. I haven't been able to find a Toastmasters class here in the wilderness that works with my schedule." So God goes theological on him. "Who made your mouth? Hmmmm? Let's see...*I* did! I will teach you what to say!"

Moses may be out of excuses, but he still hasn't told God what is on his mind. So he finally cuts to the chase. "O Lord, I just plain don't want to go to Egypt! Please send *anybody* but me!" As you might expect, God is getting ticked off, but he knows Moses is the man for the moment. So he says, "Okay, okay, I'll let you win that one. You don't have to speak. I'll appoint your brother, Aaron, to speak for you. But you're not off the hook. You still must go. And you must tell Aaron what to say."

So Moses leaves Midian with his family, meets his brother in the desert, and brings him up to speed on the burning bush conversation. Then the two of them return to Egypt, where Aaron brings God's message to the elders of Israel and Moses performs a few miracles so they will believe. And they all worship the Lord.

Can You Discover God's Plan?

It must be nice for God to speak directly to you out of a burning bush. You would never doubt who God is or what he wants you to do. But for us today, it seems different. Can we discover God's plan for our lives? If so, how?

One way to think about God's plan for your life is in macro/micro terms. At a macrolevel, God wants you to be like Jesus: courageous, humble, joyful, compassionate, patient. God's eternal and ultimate desire is for you "to be conformed to the image of his Son."[7] Whatever it takes—blessings, trials, challenges—God wants to shape you into a person who loves like Jesus. He doesn't need to tell you that over and over. It's his plan for your life.

But God also has a microplan for your life. That doesn't mean he has an opinion about what color car you should buy or which vacation location you should choose. It means he wants to guide your decisions so that they honor him. He does this primarily through prayer, Scripture, and wise friends. Through prayer, God listens to your heart's desires and gives you impressions through his still, small voice. Through Scripture, God shapes your mind with his values, so you will recognize what's good and bad in life. Through wise friends, God gives you counsel and insights that help you hear his whispers. God is still revealing his plan to all who want to know and do it.

Moses Leads Israel out of Egypt

Now in a story this good, if there's a hero like Moses, there's got to be a villain lurking in the shadows. Enter, Pharaoh Ramses II, Son of the Sun-God!

At this time in history, Egyptians believe that the sun is the most powerful of all their gods. Conveniently, they call it the Sun-God. They also believe that Pharaoh is the son of the Sun-God. In contrast, the Hebrews believe that their God is the true God. So God challenges Pharaoh to a contest. God says, "Pharaoh, I will send plagues on Egypt. See if you can stop them. Let's see who the real God is." Each plague is a direct challenge to Pharaoh's alleged powers over anything and everything in nature.

It seems like God loves this kind of contest:

> Then the LORD said to Moses, "Get up early in the morning and stand before Pharaoh. Tell him, 'This is what the LORD, the God of the Hebrews, says: Let my people go, so they can worship me. If you don't, I will send more plagues on you and your officials and your people. Then you will know that there is no one like me in all the earth. By now I could have lifted my hand and struck you and your people with a plague to wipe you off the face of the earth. But I have spared you for a purpose—to show you my power and to spread my fame throughout the earth.'"[8]

God sends nine backbreaking plagues, but Pharaoh never cries uncle. So God sends the tenth and final plague, which leads to what we call the exodus. In this final plague, God sends a death angel to kill all the firstborn sons in Egypt. But there is a caveat for the Israelites: If they will paint the doorframes of their little houses with lamb's blood from a sacrifice, then the Angel of Death will "pass over" the home. That night they obey, God spares them, and they celebrate the first Passover ever. This final plague gets Pharaoh's attention. The death of his firstborn son, the heir to his kingdom, breaks his heart. So he gives up and tells

Moses, "All right, all right. Your God wins! Now get out of town and take those crummy old Israelites with you!"

The Israelites pack up and leave Egypt, just like they are told. But they haven't been gone long before Pharaoh changes his mind and says, "Upon further reflection, maybe I was rash." Or to put it another way, "D'oh! I just lost all my free labor. Let's go get them!" So he sets out in hot pursuit after his ex-slaves. Soon the Israelites find themselves in a huge predicament. They are camped out by the Red Sea. If they advance, they will drown in the waters. If they retreat, they will be smothered by the Egyptian army. If they do nothing, they will be sitting ducks.

What would you do? I know what I would do. I would pray. Then I would look for someone to blame for my misfortune. Maybe I'm an Israelite at heart.

> As Pharaoh approached, the people of Israel looked up and panicked when they saw the Egyptians overtaking them. They cried out to the LORD, and they said to Moses, "Why did you bring us out here to die in the wilderness? Weren't there enough graves for us in Egypt?...Didn't we tell you this would happen while we were still in Egypt? We said, 'Leave us alone! Let us be slaves to the Egyptians. It's better to be a slave in Egypt than a corpse in the wilderness!'"
>
> But Moses told the people, "Don't be afraid. Just stand still and watch the LORD rescue you today. The Egyptians you see today will never be seen again. The LORD himself will fight for you. Just stay calm."[9]

As always, God keeps his word. He parts the waters, leads his people across the seafloor on dry ground, then drowns the Egyptian army when they follow.

With fresh wind in their sails of faith, the Israelites journey to the Sinai desert. Along the way, God miraculously cares for his people by placing a cloud in the sky by day and fire in the sky at night to guide them, provides water from the rock when they are thirsty, and gives manna from heaven when they are hungry.

God has finally rescued his children from slavery. But he's not finished.

GOD RESCUES ISRAEL TO RESCUE THE WORLD

God's Part

When they arrive at Mount Sinai, God meets the whole nation. Speaking out of a volcanic mountain, he renews the promise he earlier made to Abraham, then ratifies it in the form of a covenant. In this covenant, each party has a responsibility. God's part is to rescue Israel.

> Exactly two months after the Israelites left Egypt, they arrived in the wilderness of Sinai...and set up camp there at the base of Mount Sinai. Then Moses climbed the mountain to appear before God. The LORD called to him from the mountain and said, "Give these instructions to the family of Jacob; announce it to the descendants of Israel: 'You have seen what I did to the Egyptians. You know how I carried you on eagles' wings and brought you to myself.'"[10]

GRACE COMES FIRST

The next time you read the Ten Commandments in Exodus 20, remember to read the preamble in Exodus 19:1-4. It reminds us that God's grace precedes God's law. God saves before he ever commands. Grace always comes first. Only then do we have a reason to obey.

Israel's Part

God's responsibility is to rescue Israel. But Israel also has a responsibility. Her part is to represent God to all the nations.

> Now if you will obey me and keep my covenant, you will be my own special treasure from among all the peoples on earth; for all the earth belongs to me. And you will be my kingdom of priests, my holy nation.[11]

All the nations in the world belong to God. Yet God chooses Israel for a special purpose. Not to be a political powerhouse, but to be a kingdom of priests. A priest serves as a bridge between God and humans. Remember chapter 2 in God's Great Story? Here's the promise God made to Abram:

> I will make you into a great nation. I will bless you and make you famous, and you will be a blessing to others. I will bless those who bless you and curse those who treat you with contempt. All the families on earth will be blessed through you."[12]

God wants his chosen people not to revel in their chosenness, but to represent him to all people everywhere.

This brings us to the centerpiece of the covenant: The Ten Commandments. They are God's way of saying, "I expect you to live in such a way that you are different from all the nations around you. Let me spell out what I mean in ten clear commands."[13]

The Ten Commandments summarize how Israel is to live a qualitatively different life than her neighbors. The first four commands are vertical: "No other gods before me, no images of me, no name above my name, no day above my day." The fifth command is both vertical and horizontal: "Obey your parents, because they represent me." The last five commands are horizontal—that is, social and outward-facing: "Don't take someone's life, don't take someone's husband or wife, don't take someone's possessions, don't fudge on the truth, don't crave what others have."

If the Israelites will obey those commands, then they will look radically different from the pagan nations around them. And the nations will say, "We want to serve the God you serve!" That is the best way Israel can ever show God's character to the world.

Look again at the pattern in this chapter: God rescues Moses, so Moses can rescue Israel, so Israel can rescue the world. God does not rescue Moses for his sake, or Israel for her sake. He rescues both for the world's sake.

That is still God's pattern.

SLAVE OR FREE?

By grace, God rescues you. Through the sacrificial death and triumphant resurrection of Jesus, you are made free. The question is…are you living free?

- Are you enjoying being God's son or daughter and loving him as your heavenly Father?

- Are you eagerly following Jesus every day, learning from him how to live in God's Kingdom?

- Are you keeping in step with the Spirit, who fills you with his love, joy, and peace?

Or are you enslaved to something?

- Is it alcohol, sexual images, or drugs?

- What about food, pride, or work?

- Maybe people-pleasing, electronic devices, or money?

None of these things is evil in and of itself. In the beginning, God created nothing evil. Everything God made was good because God is good. But because sin is evil, every good thing has been twisted or distorted. What God intended for good, the evil one disfigured. Every heavenly gift now has a hellish shadow-side.

These twisted gifts fight for your attention. They compete for your allegiance. They struggle for your soul. And they aren't satisfied until you fall on your knees and worship them with all your heart, soul, mind, and strength. When that happens, they have become your gods. They are your idols. They own you.

WHO IS YOUR MASTER?

From past experience, you know that anything that owns you is your master—and usually a cruel one. Think about how ruthless sex can be as a false god. Or money. Or alcohol. They don't want to influence you for good. They want to lead you down the path to ruin. None of these idols are good rulers. When they are lord of your life, they are not kind and loving. They are demonic and destructive. Jesus wants to save you from every idol that masquerades as a sheep in wolf's clothing. Turn to the only Lord who is worthy of your life and love. Let Jesus rescue you from your false gods.

As with Moses, God doesn't rescue you simply for your sake. He rescues you so that you can rescue others. Of course, when we say *rescue*, we don't mean the codependent kind of rescuing where you feel responsible for someone's happiness and then rescue them out of false guilt or foolish fear. We mean the kind of rescuing that arises from a heart of joy before God. The kind of rescuing that comes from a God-given desire to serve others.

WHOM IS GOD CALLING
YOU TO RESCUE?

Does God want you to be a foster family for children who have never known a healthy home?

Is the Lord asking you to ally your energies with an agency that fights sex-trafficking?

Are you being called to go into prisons or halfway houses to show God's mercy and teach God's truth?

God has not rescued you for your sake alone. You have been saved to serve. You have been rescued so you can be a rescuer. That is what chapter 3 in God's Great Story means to your story.

THE STORY BETWEEN THE STORY

One day while Moses is on Mount Sinai with God, the children of Israel go totally bonkers. In a classic act of people-pleasing, Aaron leads them in worshipping a golden calf, which ends badly for all involved. Moses gets angry, breaks the stone tablets, sees the Lord's glory, gets a second set of tablets, and goes down the mountain with a bunch of laws so these sinful people will know how to live with a holy God.

Always faithful, God delivers his people right to the doorstep of an awesome new land, but they freak out over the big, nasty locals and say they'd rather go back to Egypt than trust the God who delivered them out of slavery in the first place. As punishment, the children of Israel wander in the wilderness for forty years until they all die off, except for Joshua and Caleb, who never doubted God's goodness.

After Moses dies, God raises up Joshua as the new leader of his people and gives him the green light to take the Promised Land. Stories of God's power and glory have the big, nasty locals quaking in their boots, and with the help of an unlikely ally named Rahab, the children of Israel finally cross the Jordan River, take the city of Jericho, and enter the Promised Land, just like God intended forty years prior.

The next few hundred years are a cycle of backsliding, defeat, and God's gracious deliverance of his hardheaded, hard-hearted people. God provides judges to help deliver them, including Deborah, Gideon, and Samuel. Never satisfied, the children of Israel want to be like the cool kids and have a monarchy, so God relents and gives them King Saul, who proves they really should be careful what they wish for.

And that, in a nutshell, is the story between the story.

Deborah   **Gideon**   **Samuel**

JUDGES ARE LAME!

CAN WE HAVE A KING INSTEAD?

King Saul   **King David**

4

GOD CHOOSES

I n every pundit's eye, Saul was the number one draft choice to be the first king of Israel. He had all the measurables the Israelites were looking for— tall, strong, and straight out of central casting. Unfortunately, he didn't have the intangibles. He was insecure, impatient, and given to fits of jealous rage. Not a good combination for the potentate of a start-up nation having to fend off a relentless enemy. Needless to say, he was a huge bust.[1]

To clean up the mess, God sends Samuel, his GM at the time, to Bethlehem to sign a diamond-in-the-rough-prospect—one of Jesse's boys. The trouble is, Jesse has eight of them. Samuel is totally surprised when God doesn't give the thumbs-up to Eliab, the firstborn. After the Lord passes on the next six, a flustered Samuel asks Jesse about number eight. Turns out he's on the back forty tending the sheep. Samuel tells Jesse he'd be happy to wait, and when David finally arrives, God makes it clear to Samuel that David is his choice to lead his people.

In that moment, Samuel plucks David out of the relative obscurity of rural Bethlehem and sets him on the fast track to stardom. A thumbnail sketch of David's life looks like this:

- There are moments of glorious victory, like felling Goliath, returning the ark of the covenant to Jerusalem, and leading the nation of Israel to unprecedented heights.

- Followed by moments of ignominious shame as seen in the Bathsheba affair—the seduction of a married beauty and murder of her loyal husband to cover his tracks.

- And finally, he is overwhelmed by gut-wrenching sorrow. His parental neglect leads to his son Absalom's mutinous choice to overthrow him. Riding into battle against his father's men, Absalom forgets to put his hair in a man bun and gets his luxuriant locks caught in a low-hanging branch. As he's dangling helplessly in a tree, David's general puts three daggers in his heart...and he might as well have put one in David's too, for David's beloved Absalom is dead.

David is pretty much a lame duck from then on—about the only good thing he does after that is crown his son Solomon the next king...and that's David's chapter in God's Great Story! Check out the official version here.[2]

GOD'S STORY

In David's chapter, God is unveiling something significant about himself. What it is may surprise you at first, but as the Great Story goes along, you'll see God doing it again and again. What is it?

GOD OFTEN CHOOSES THE LEAST EXPECTED

As God's Great Story unfolds, you're going to see that he has a pattern of choosing the least expected persons to do some of his most important work. If you spent even a minute in Vacation Bible School as a kid, you've seen a depiction of the shepherd boy who grows up to be a man "after [God's] own heart."[3] So to suggest that David is the poster child for God choosing the least expected to accomplish his divine purposes may come as a shock. The truth is David already has two strikes against him, and all things being equal, his contemporaries would have fully expected God to skip right over him and pick someone else to be Saul's successor.

David Flunked the Birth Order Test

"Primogeniture" is the fancy word for "the firstborn son wins the lottery." In antiquity, the firstborn son was considered the crown prince of the family. He would have authority over the family in the event of the father's death.[4] He also received a double portion of the inheritance. In essence, he was next to rule the roost. Primogeniture was not simply a cultural suggestion; it was the "linchpin of the entire social and legal system put in place to define the rights and privileges of everyone in the culture."[5] To fail to honor this societal law was to disrupt the social order and, needless to say, was highly frowned upon. And yet, as God's Great Story unfolds, he repeatedly disrupts the settled order of his people by ignoring this law and choosing a second, or even worse, a last-born son to come up onto center stage to play the leading role in some of his most iconic work.

This is why Samuel is stunned when God doesn't have him tap Eliab on the shoulder as the new king that hot afternoon in Bethlehem. As a matter of fact, this law accounts for why Jesse doesn't even think to include David in the lineup to meet with Samuel in the first place. He is the youngest—and the least in the community's eyes.

God's penchant to disrupt people's expectations about who he calls to lead is at the heart of much of the drama in the Great Story. When you have time, read about Ishmael and Isaac, Esau and Jacob, Joseph and Reuben. Jesus even reflects the prevalence of this cultural expectation in the parable of the prodigal son, and in his often quoted but rarely understood axiom, "the last shall be first, and the first [shall be] last."[6] All this to say, when Samuel anoints David as the new king, it is a total surprise to everyone who is there that day!

David Has Character Issues

Softly and tenderly, I want to help you take off any Sunday school glasses you still might be wearing to help you see that at best, David was a very complicated man. That's a nice way of saying at times he was a very bad man. "Bathsheba-gate," as the Jews might call it today, was just the tip of the iceberg. He could be incredibly ruthless, vindictive, and violent; and, he had a very long memory.

For example, take the case of Shimei. On the lam from Absalom, David rides into a small town where Shimei throws rocks and curses at him. One of Saul's clan, Shimei has bought the family line that David stole Saul's throne as opposed to God giving it to him. Now that Absalom is trying to take it from David, Shimei is relishing the fact that somebody is giving him a taste of his own medicine. One of David's men asks if he should go and separate Shimei's head from his body, but David deescalates the situation by suggesting that perhaps God is in it.

After Absalom's death, David is restored to his kingship. Shimei is among the first to congratulate him and asks David to forgive him for the terrible things he had said. Aghast at Shimei's audacity, another one of David's men offers to put a quick end to Shimei and his wayward tongue. Once again, David says no, this is a day of celebration not execution, and he promises Shimei his life will be spared.

Apparently, though, David had his fingers crossed when he says this, because on his deathbed he gives his son and successor, Solomon, the "famous last words" speech. It's the expected "obey the Lord and keep his covenant and all will go well with you" speech. David also encourages Solomon to be good to the people who had been good to him. Nice. But then he whispers these final words, "I swore by the Lord that I would not kill [Shimei]. But that oath does not make him innocent. You are a wise man, and you will know how to arrange a bloody death for him." Then he breathes his last. Yikes…talk about holding a grudge. And this is the guy who wrote most of the book of Psalms![7] When it comes to David, Aleksandr Solzhenitsyn couldn't be more correct: "The line dividing good and evil cuts through the heart of every human being."[8]

Still, God uses David to unify the twelve tribes of Israel, usher in unsurpassed national prosperity, and renew the worship life of his people. David's reign is such a glorious point in Israel's history that God, through the prophet Nathan, tells him that one day a king from his line will establish a Kingdom that will never end.[9] A thousand years later, when a baby is born in Bethlehem, the fulfillment of that prophecy begins.

Don't miss this. God orchestrates all of these things through the last-born son of a small-town sheep rancher, whose life would be rated "R" for explicit sex and violence. Surprising? Yes, but David wasn't the first, and won't be the last suspicious character that God is going to use in a mighty way in his Great Story!

GOD USES A DIFFERENT
STANDARD OF JUDGMENT

When it comes to choosing leaders, God uses a different standard of judgment. If you take off the Sunday school glasses and see the real David, it raises a lot of questions. The most obvious one is, "How could God use a guy who seems so flawed, so broken, so...well, immoral?" The answer to that question is two-part. First, if God is only looking for perfect humans to partner with, he's going to be flying solo for a very long time. So he decides to do the best he can with who he's got. Second, God sees something in David that puts him at the top of his draft board. That something is David's heart.

The writer of 1 Samuel says as much when Samuel is in Bethlehem and Jesse's sons are lined up in front of him. God whispers and reminds him that he's not looking for the measurables but for the intangibles. Here's how Samuel recalls it, "Don't judge by his appearance or height, for I have rejected him. The LORD doesn't see things the way you see them. People judge by outward appearance, but the LORD looks at the heart."[10] What is it about David's heart that pleases God? A more thorough reading of David's story reveals three aspects of his heart that convince God he is the man for this moment in his Great Story.

God Chooses People Who Tenaciously Trust Him

When Israel is cowering at the feet of Goliath, no one is willing to step up and take the challenge except the underaged shepherd son of Jesse. At first Saul is skeptical that this idealistic teenager even has a chance against the Philistine MMA champion. David convinces Saul, however, with an impassioned plea:

> I have been taking care of my father's sheep and goats. When a lion or bear comes to steal a lamb from the flock, I go after it with a club and rescue the lamb from its mouth. If the animal turns on me, I catch it by the jaw and club it to death. I have done this to both lions and bears, and I'll do it to this pagan Philistine, too, for he has defied the armies of the living God! The Lord who rescued me from the claws of the lion and the bear will rescue me from this Philistine![11]

Love and forgiveness are given, but trust is earned. God clearly has earned David's trust by faithfully helping him put together an undefeated record against the local bears and lions. So the thought of taking on a lumbering giant in an open field is no big deal to David.

Some of the best trash-talking you'll ever read can be found in 1 Samuel 17 as David engages Goliath. The big palooka is offended when Israel sends out a pipsqueak kid to face him. "Am I a dog...that you come at me with a stick?" he roars, adding the requisite Philistine curse words.[12] Unfazed, David yells back something like, "You come at me with your puny weapons, but I've got the Lord of Heaven's Armies on my side. I'm going to kill you and cut off your head, and then my bros here are going to feed the dead carcasses of the rest of your friends to the vultures so that when the day is done the whole world will know that there is a God in Israel! Bring it!" Perhaps you know how the story ends. One well-aimed projectile from David's sling hits Goliath right between the eyes, and David and the rest of his Israelite clan carry out his prophetic pre-game rant.

David tenaciously trusts God because God had proven himself to be faithful to David for as long as he could remember. As the writer of the book of Hebrews will one day write, "Without faith it is impossible to please God."[13] This being the case, no wonder God is drawn to David—he has buckets full of faith.

God Chooses People Who Have a Soft Heart

Anyone who wields as much power and participates in as much bloodshed, betrayal, and brutality as David does can easily become hardened—emotionally, relationally, and spiritually. Simple survival of the self requires the deft use of denial, blame-shifting, rationalization, and defensiveness. Despite Saul's toxic jealousy, Absalom's attempted coup, and his own lusty shenanigans, David's heart, more often than not, remains soft toward God.

Case in point—Bathshebagate.[14] Not only does David misuse his power to have his way with and impregnate a young married subject, he then conspires to cover up his dirty deed, which tragically leads to the murder of Uriah, her husband. Not good. Clearly David had never heard that "it's not the crime, it's the cover up" that will get you every time.[15]

Before long the prophet Nathan comes knocking on David's door. Knowing how busy David is, Nathan asks if can tell him a quick story. Two men lived in a certain town. One was rich and had scads of sheep and cattle. The other was poor and owned nothing but a little lamb. That little lamb was precious to the man. It ate from his plate and drank from his cup. The man cuddled the lamb like it was his own child. One day a guest arrived at the home of the rich man. Unthinkably, instead of taking a lamb—that he would never miss—from his own flock, he took the poor man's lamb, killed it, smoked it on his big green egg, and fed it to his guest.

By now David is seething! "Any man who would do something like that deserves to die!" Nathan lets that phrase hang in the air for a moment, and then with impeccable timing says, "David, you are that man!" Nathan goes on, unnecessarily, filling in the details, but David knows: He is the rich man. Uriah was the poor man. And he not only stole his wife, he stole his life.

What comes next is astounding. David offers no excuses. He doesn't shift the blame to Bathsheba for taking a bath in the palace pool in broad daylight. He doesn't make one of his generals the scapegoat. He doesn't try to rationalize that given all he has done for Israel, he deserves a little fringe benefit. No, he owns it. He simply confesses, "I have sinned against the Lord."[16]

The depth of his godly sorrow for this sin is on full display for anyone to read. It is the inspiration for one of the most profound psalms of confession. Here it is, in part:

> Have mercy on me, O God, because of your unfailing love. Because of your great compassion, blot out the stain of my sins. Wash me clean from my guilt. Purify me from my sin. For I recognize my rebellion; it haunts me day and night. Against you, and you alone, have I sinned; I have done what is evil in your sight. You will be proved right in what you say, and your judgment against me is just...
>
> Purify me from my sins, and I will be clean; wash me, and I will be whiter than snow...Create in me a clean heart, O God.

> Renew a loyal spirit within me. Do not banish me from your
> presence, and don't take your Holy Spirit from me.
>
> Restore to me the joy of your salvation, and make me
> willing to obey you. Then I will teach your ways to rebels, and
> they will return to you...
>
> You do not desire a sacrifice, or I would offer one. You do
> not want a burnt offering. The sacrifice you desire is a broken
> spirit. You will not reject a broken and repentant heart,
> O God.[17]

What kind of man with this much power, who answers to no other man, would respond in this way? What kind of man could write such a poignant confession? Only a man who kept his heart soft toward God. The secret to David's rich and enduring relationship with God is this: Although he was a really big sinner, he had a really soft heart.

God Chooses People Who Have a Deep Inner Life

When you read the psalms of David, you notice right away that he is passionate, confessional, and often painfully honest. At other times, his words reflect breathtaking awe, overwhelming wonder, reverential fear, and ecstatic praise. It makes you wonder what kind of relationship with God would give rise to sentiments like these that run the gamut of human emotion.

There is a deep knowing that is present, but the transcendent majesty of God is not lost in the familiar. Whatever else might be said about this relationship, it was cultivated over the course of much time and attention.

Surely it began when David was a shepherd boy. A shepherd's life was, as the adage says, months of boredom punctuated by moments of sheer terror. What did shepherds do to occupy themselves with all that down time? There was no internet, no smartphone, no ESPN, no podcasts, no TED Talks, not even a Bible. Only craggy hills, green pastures, starry skies, and an occasional wild animal or two. And, oh yes, God.

Evidently David took advantage of the time and devoted his attention to getting to know God. Speaking, listening, writing, reflecting, singing, and dancing all come forth when you get to know the One who made it all. After a while, words like these just come flowing out of the heart and soul:

> O LORD, you have examined my heart
>> and know everything about me.
> You know when I sit down or stand up.
>> You know my thoughts even when I'm far away.
> You see me when I travel
>> and when I rest at home.
>> You know everything I do.
> You know what I am going to say
>> even before I say it, LORD.
> You go before me and follow me.
>> You place your hand of blessing on my head.
> Such knowledge is too wonderful for me,
>> too great for me to understand![18]

And here's the other side of the coin. God got to know David too. That's what David is celebrating in the lines from Psalm 139 above. In David's day, the gods of the other tribes surrounding the Israelites weren't all that interested in people. In fact, people were considered a nuisance and quite a bother. The thought of a god being interested in and caring about a single human being was unheard of. It's in the wilderness, though, with time on his hands, and distractions at a minimum, that it dawns on David that God wants to know him too. Really know him—experientially, personally, in real time. And know him he did…all his strengths and weaknesses, gifts and flaws, selflessness and selfishness. With full knowledge of it all, God loved him, blessed him, and invited him into his grand adventure all the same.

Here's some really good news. God has full knowledge of your life. All of it. Start to finish. Good and bad. And yes, he is inviting you into his epic story too. That may come as a huge surprise, knowing yourself the way you do. You may feel like you were born at the wrong place in the birth order, at the wrong time in history, or even in the wrong place, period. Your character issues may flash red in your head like a blinking light at a four-way stop. But if God can choose a man like David, he can choose you to write a brand-new chapter in his ongoing Story of redemption. It is important to note, however, that while David had a long list of major sins and other peccadillos, the three qualities highlighted above were essential for God's ongoing work in and through him to happen.

ARE YOU TRUSTING GOD LIKE DAVID?

Tenacious trust is the foundation for any relationship—especially your relationship with God. As long as David trusted that God was with him and for him, the door to his heart and soul remained open to God's presence, blessing, and correction. He was still malleable in God's hands. God could use him for his strategic purposes in the lives of his people.

The same can be said of you. The place to start is believing that God is for you and with you. Resting in the assurance that he is always working for your good in every situation motivates you to trust him, follow him, and obey him. When you do, God knows that he can trust you too. So…he puts your number on speed dial…and opportunities to do his work in the world will abound.

IS YOUR HEART
SOFT TOWARD GOD?

We must also remember that the best of intentions will not immunize us against random acts of stupidity. Like the apostle Paul confessed, "I want to do what is right, but I can't. I want to do what is good, but I don't. I don't want to do what is wrong, but I do it anyway…Oh, what a miserable person I am!"[19] Evidently this is the human lot. This is why David's example of a soft heart is so crucial. God's preference is that we make wise decisions 24/7. Since we don't, though, what matters next is how we respond. Will we pridefully harden our hearts and insist that we couldn't possibly have done anything wrong? Will we point the finger of blame at an innocent or unsuspecting foil? Will we chalk it up to bad parenting or the lack of positive role models in our formative years? Or, like David, will we turn to God with a sorrowful heart, confessing our failures, seeking forgiveness, and yearning to be restored to our place in his world? Soft heart, we're back in God's game. Hard heart, we're out.

ARE YOU CULTIVATING A
DEEP INNER LIFE WITH GOD?

This may be the toughest spiritual challenge we face today. We no longer live in a pastoral setting, spending hours under the stars soaking up the glory of nature. We've got the lure of cell phones, social media, and bingeable content at our fingertips. There's hardly any bandwidth left for God. We need the inspiration of Christian contemplatives from days gone by to remind us that we cannot develop a deep inner life with God in the past, for those days are locked behind doors that can never be opened again. Neither can we cultivate a deep relationship with God in the future. Those are doors yet to be opened. The only moment in which we can truly get to know God intimately is the present moment. So, like David, seek to live every moment of every day with a confident awareness that God is your constant, unseen companion. Whisper words to him. Listen for his voice. Keep David's words, recorded in Psalms, running through your mind. Allow them to flow down into your heart. Draw strength from God and fearlessly slay the giants standing between you and the life he intends for you.

If you can do these three things, one day it will be said of you, like David, "Now when David had served God's purpose in his own generation, he fell asleep..."[20]

Lord, may it be so for each of us.

THE STORY BETWEEN THE STORY

While David is a great king and a man after God's own heart, his family is *crazy* dysfunctional. After David's death, his son Solomon is chosen by God to lead the nation, and God blesses him with great wisdom. It's an age of peace and prosperity for Israel. But despite his wisdom, Solomon buys into the lie that more is better, taking 700 wives and 300 concubines. And then he buys into the lie that what's good for the goose is good for the gander, and he worships many of their false gods.

After Solomon's death it's pretty much all downhill for Israel as a civil war ends in a divided nation. The northern kingdom keeps the name Israel, while the southern kingdom takes the name Judah, and a procession of weak and idolatrous kings rule both kingdoms in the years that follow. For example, King Ahab of Israel marries a foreign woman named Jezebel. As you might guess from her name, Jezebel is *not* a nice lady. Under her influence, King Ahab builds altars to the fertility gods Baal and Asherah, encouraging God's people to worship these false gods. This is a decision that ends badly for just about everyone.

Through the years, God sends prophets like Elijah, Elisha, and Isaiah to remind the people of God's faithful love and warn them of the consequences of their sin. But the people love their false gods way too much to listen to the one true God. Time after time, despite the warning of the prophets, the beloved children of Israel mercilessly break the heart of God. Because of their stubborn disobedience, God finally allows his people to experience his judgment.

And that, in a nutshell, is the story between the story.

GOD WARNS

Wealth advisors have a saying, "The first generation makes it, the second generation spends it, and the third generation blows it." Enter David. He amasses generational wealth, power, and political unity for Israel. His son Solomon spends it. And his grandson Rehoboam blows it. Rehoboam makes one decision after another, which undermines everything David accomplished and starts the nation of Israel on a downward spiral to political and spiritual oblivion. Within 343 years, God's people no longer exist as a national entity, and their spiritual life lies in tatters.[1] The northern kingdom, called Israel, is obliterated by the Assyrians in 722 BC. Judah, the southern kingdom, is overtaken by the Babylonians in 586 BC, and most of its citizens are shipped 900 miles away[2] into exile in Babylon.

Evidently, no matter how many things change through the centuries, some things remain the same.

God is not standing idly by, however, while all of this is going on. He continually sends a host of eclectic characters, a.k.a. prophets, as his official spokespersons to remind his people of the promises and sanctions in their covenant agreement made first with Abraham and reconfirmed with Moses. Here's the short version, "If you obey you will prosper. If you disobey you will perish." The longer version can be found in Deuteronomy 28:1-68. The first fourteen verses tell all the lavish ways God will bless his people if they obey. The last fifty-four verses describe in lurid detail the sanctions and consequences they can expect if they are disobedient and turn away from him. Let's just say it's not for the faint of heart. It will get so bad to be an Israelite that when God gets through with them, they are going to be willing to sell themselves into slavery, but no one will be buying.

The way the Old Testament (think "old covenant") lays it out, God is a velvet brick—a little bit of velvet, a whole lot of brick. But out of his loving-kindness he sends prophets to give his people ample warning to get back on track before all the unpleasantness kicks in. While this description may sound harsh, God doesn't have a quick trigger. In fact, he's astoundingly patient. He gives Israel 208 years to get its act together. He gives Judah an additional 136. So it is into this dysfunctional political and spiritual mess that God sends a gallery of colorful spokespersons to try to talk some sense into them.

To better understand how God seeks to nudge the storyline of his people in a more faithful direction, it's important to clear up some misunderstandings about the prophets. Most often we think they are prognosticators of future events, which is correct. The trouble is our focus tends to be on events like the coming of Jesus or the end times, which have no connection to the people and circumstances that the prophets were addressing.

When you break it down, less than 2 percent of Old Testament prophecy is messianic. Less than 1 percent refers to events yet to come in our lifetime. In light of this, one Old Testament scholar concludes, "The prophets *did* indeed announce the future. But it was usually the immediate future of Israel, Judah, and other nations surrounding them that they announced rather than *our* future. One of the keys to understanding the prophets, therefore, is that for us to see their prophecies fulfilled, we must look back on times that for them were still future but for us are past."[3] With these thoughts in mind, let's explore how God uses the prophets in his Great Story.

PROPHETS ARE AN EARLY WARNING SYSTEM

The Purpose of the Prophets

Most of us know about and depend on armed forces using high-tech military satellite warning systems and meteorologists wielding doppler radars to keep us safe. It's their job to be fully aware of the current conditions of everything going on around them, identify any threats coming over the horizon, and apprise the public of what they will need to do to survive—shelter in place, evacuate, or run for cover. While significantly lower tech, prophets carried out much the same function. God gave them unusual discernment. They could read between the lines of their culture and know the condition of people's hearts, their communities, and their nation as a whole. More importantly, they also could predict when a holy storm front was on the way and then communicate to people what they needed to do not just to survive, but to thrive in their covenant relationship with God.

A Quick Look at the Prophets

God casts the roles of his official spokespersons with a list of unusual characters throughout Old Testament history. Fifteen of the prophets authored books in the Old Testament beginning with Isaiah and ending with Malachi.[4] There are, however, more individuals designated in the Old Testament as prophets, most of whom do not have any prophetic writing attributed to them. For example, there was Moses, who liberated the children of Israel from Egyptian slavery; Samuel, who led the people during the period of the Judges; Nathan, who guided David; and Elijah of Mount Carmel fame. While it is often overlooked, five women are identified as prophets—Miriam, Deborah, Huldah, the wife of Isaiah (who might have been Huldah), and Noadiah.[5]

Of the fifteen prophetic books listed in the Old Testament, three—Isaiah, Jeremiah, and Ezekiel—are designated as major prophets. The other twelve have been labeled as minor prophets. Don't let this fool you. It doesn't mean only three were good enough to make it to the big leagues while the others were destined to be stuck in AA. The major prophets wrote full-length sermons, while the minor ones wrote more devotional-length messages.

Here's a thumbnail sketch of a few of them. Isaiah (circa 740 BC), perhaps of royal stock, was an urbanite from Jerusalem who floated effortlessly among the elite. He likely was accused of taking his prophetic role a bit too far because he named his sons with a prophetic twist—Shear-jashub, which means "a remnant shall return," Immanuel, which means "God with us," and finally Maher-Shalal-Hash-Baz, the longest name in the Old Testament, which means "spoil quickly, plunder speedily," a heads-up about the impending invasion of the Assyrians.

Jeremiah (circa 626 BC) rarely made the guest list for a party of any kind. A real "Dougie-downer," Jeremiah denounced just about everyone and everything around him, even God at one point for getting him into this line of work in the first place.[6] He smashed pots and cried a lot. He got so tired of God's people breaking their covenant agreement that when God told him one day he was going to nix the whole thing and establish a new one, he could hardly contain himself. More on that later in the story.

Then there's Hosea (circa 755 BC), perhaps the most interesting prophet of all. While prophets normally communicated their messages in speeches—or oracles, as they were called—Hosea's message was delivered as a living parable. God told him to marry a woman who was more comfortable hanging out at a strip joint than the Temple. Anyone with half a brain could see where this story was heading. Gomer delivered three kids in quick succession, but before they were all out of diapers, she headed out the door and returned to her former life. Long story short, God told Hosea to chase her down, pay the buy-out to release her from a very unfortunate contract, and bring her home. Which he did. When one reads Hosea's story, it's easy to see the parallels between God and his people and Hosea and Gomer.

These three prophets, along with the other twelve, are used by God to warn his people of a coming judgment if they do not come to their senses and turn their hearts back to him. To fully grasp the nature of God and the story he was writing through the prophets, it's imperative to have a clear understanding of the essential message they were tasked to communicate.

GOD COMMUNICATES A CONSISTENT MESSAGE

The Prophets Indict God's People

If you were to compile a list of Israel's and Judah's sins noted by the prophets, it would be long and lusty. Their pursuit of money, sex, power, and all their trappings would make Vegas blush. Their insatiable appetites for more led them down the path of following other gods, like Baal the fertility god, in hopes that the "more" they were looking for could be supplied in even greater abundance. Unfortunately for them, this path dead ends at the intersection of idolatry and social injustice—two of God's biggest no-no's.

Here's an example of one prophet's message that will give you a sense of how God expresses his displeasure with his people:

> Hear the word of the LORD, O people of Israel!
> The LORD has brought charges against you, saying:
> "There is no faithfulness, no kindness,
>   no knowledge of God in your land.
> You make vows and break them;
>   you kill and steal and commit adultery.
> There is violence everywhere—
>   one murder after another.
> That is why your land is in mourning,
>   and everyone is wasting away.
> Even the wild animals, the birds of the sky,
>   and the fish of the sea are disappearing."[7]

When you read these prophets, it's clear that God takes sin seriously. In the overwhelming majority of prophetic texts, his judgment seems emotionally detached, direct, even cold. Then, as now, people who are caught up in sinful behavior tend to experience him as a brick. On the other hand, there are a few passages where the velvet comes out and you get the feeling that God is not as incensed as he is heartbroken.

> Therefore, go and give this message to Israel. This is what the
> LORD says:
>
>> "O Israel, my faithless people,
>>> come home to me again,
>> for I am merciful.
>>> I will not be angry with you forever.
>> Only acknowledge your guilt...
>> And I will give you shepherds after my own heart,
>>> who will guide you with knowledge and understanding."[8]

The Prophets Warn of Future Consequences

Upon pronouncing Israel's or Judah's guilt, the prophets then foretell the consequences that await those who have turned their backs on God and his covenant. The purpose of these predictions about their future is to change their thoughts and behaviors in the present. Simply put, the prophets held out the possibility of a stick or a carrot. Those who refused to repent and turn back to God would get smacked with judgment. Those who did repent got a promise of salvation and blessing:

> This is what the LORD of Heaven's Armies, the God of Israel,
> says:
>> "Even now, if you quit your evil ways, I will let you stay in
>> your own land. But don't be fooled by those who promise you

> safety simply because the Lord's Temple is here. They chant,
> 'The Lord's Temple is here! The Lord's Temple is here!' But I
> will be merciful only if you stop your evil thoughts and deeds
> and start treating each other with justice; only if you stop
> exploiting foreigners, orphans, and widows; only if you stop
> your murdering; and only if you stop harming yourselves by
> worshiping idols. Then I will let you stay in this land that I gave
> to your ancestors to keep forever."[9]

Don't miss the point of this and other predictions. The predictions are not expressing what God wants to happen. Rather, they are intended to motivate his people to change their behavior so the worst *won't* happen.[10] If a financial advisor tells a client to stop running up the balance on his credit card or he will end up in bankruptcy, that is a prophetic prediction. The advisor's objective is to get the client to change his extravagant ways so that he won't experience bankruptcy. God's purpose in warning his people of impending judgment through his prophets is always redemptive, not punitive.

The Prophets Promise Hope

In a sense God is the originator of tough love. Speaking through Jeremiah, God reminds his people that he has loved them with an everlasting love.[11] Allowing them to experience the full weight of the consequences of their sin is his last resort. Nations, like individuals, often have to hit bottom before they will think to look up again. But when they do, God will be ready to welcome them back— and it will be a new day!

In spite of how often God's people chase after other gods, his love is longsuffering, and he longs for the day when they will return to him and live again in the lap of his goodness. Each prophet, in his own place and time, holds out a beautiful vision of what redemption and restoration will look like. Here is a hope-giving example from the prophet Jeremiah:

> "In that day," says the LORD, "I will be the God of all the families of Israel, and they will be my people. This is what the LORD says:
>
>> "Those who survive the coming destruction
>>> will find blessings even in the barren land,
>>> for I will give rest to the people of Israel."
>> Long ago the LORD said to Israel:
>> "I have loved you, my people, with an everlasting love.
>>> With unfailing love I have drawn you to myself.
>> I will rebuild you, my virgin Israel.
>>> You will again be happy
>>> and dance merrily with your tambourines.
>> Again you will plant your vineyards on the mountains
>>> of Samaria
>>> and eat from your own gardens there.
>> The day will come when watchmen will shout
>>> from the hill country of Ephraim,
>> 'Come, let us go up to Jerusalem
>>> to worship the LORD our God.'"[12]

The sad truth about the prophets during this period is that no matter how many times they "rinse and repeat" the tough-love cycle, the hearts of the people do not change. When God called Israel to be his chosen people, he had high hopes for his relationship with them and their success in becoming an instrument of blessing for all nations. Unfortunately, as time went on, it became apparent that Israel was not going to live up to its part of the bargain.

Early in Isaiah's ministry, God expresses his growing frustration with his people by using the metaphor of a vineyard. He had wanted to create a vineyard that by comparison would make Napa Valley look like Death Valley. He cleared and cultivated the land. Planted the finest vines. Built a state-of-the-art security tower and wine press. When the harvest came, he was expecting sweet, mouthwatering grapes. Instead, what he got were sour grapes that set his teeth on edge. Almost in exasperation God asks, "What more could I have done for my vineyard that I have not already done?"[13]

It turns out that God answers his own question by promising to do two new things. First, he is going to send a Messiah, an anointed one who will save his people and create a new kingdom of people, a new Israel, if you will. Perhaps you are familiar with Isaiah's description of the coming one:

> For a child is born to us,
>   a son is given to us.
> The government will rest on his shoulders.
>   And he will be called:
> Wonderful Counselor, Mighty God,
>   Everlasting Father, Prince of Peace.
> His government and its peace
>   will never end.
> He will rule with fairness and justice from the throne of
>   his ancestor David
>   for all eternity.
> The passionate commitment of the Lord of Heaven's Armies
>   will make this happen![14]

Along with this new Messiah who will save his people, God will establish a new covenant. The covenant with Moses was flawed from the beginning. While God's faithfulness was never in doubt, the grip of sin on God's people is so tight that they would never be able to fulfill their part of the agreement. The writer of the book of Hebrews in the New Testament quotes Jeremiah's prophetic announcement of a new covenant and then explains the "why" behind God's actions:

> If the first covenant had been faultless, there would have been
> no need for a second covenant to replace it. But when God
> found fault with the people, he said:
>
> "The day is coming, says the LORD,
>   when I will make a new covenant
>   with the people of Israel and Judah....
> But this is the new covenant I will make
>   with the people of Israel on that day, says the LORD:
> I will put my laws in their minds,
>   and I will write them on their hearts.
> I will be their God,
>   and they will be my people.
> And they will not need to teach their neighbors,
>   nor will they need to teach their relatives,
>   saying, 'You should know the LORD.'
> For everyone, from the least to the greatest,
>   will know me already.
> And I will forgive their wickedness,
>   and I will never again remember their sins."

When God speaks of a "new" covenant, it means he has made the first one obsolete. It is now out of date and will soon disappear.[15]

The covenant God made with Israel through Moses was indeed gracious—the Lord rescued his people from slavery in Egypt. It was, however, conditional. Israel received the benefits of the covenant only if they were faithful. If they disobeyed, they paid. Biblical history shows that God's people were unable to live up to their promises. Perhaps this reveals the deepest flaw in the Mosaic covenant: It could not ultimately transform the hearts of those who were a part of the covenant community so that they could keep it. As a result, this covenant would become null and void. As one writer says, it had a "built-in obsolescence."[16]

The new covenant, on the other hand, is significantly different. Its scope is widened. It is between God and all peoples, not just Israel. It will be mediated through Jesus, the Messiah, who will fulfill all the covenant obligations on behalf of all people. Therefore, it is unconditional, and grace begins to flow down from heaven on all of us! That is incredibly good news and is the catalyst for the next chapter in God's Great Story—and what a chapter it is!

But first...

As I noted at the beginning of this chapter, no matter how many things change through the centuries, some things remain the same. That certainly goes for us as well. We are living 2,700 years after the prophets' words were recorded, but if you update the names and places, our stories aren't much different from the ones that evoke the oracles of long ago.

OUR CULTURE LURES US INTO IDOLATRY

Marketing experts tell us we see an average of 4,000 ads each day. They can be in the form of print ads, brand labels, Facebook and Google ads, television, radio, and other digital spaces. Ads are designed to gain our attention, trigger a sense of need, and then provide an emotional reward for buying the product that develops an ongoing craving. No wonder we buy in to the notion that our ultimate well-being and fulfillment will be found in the abundance of material things— money, sex, power, portfolios, status, homes, cars, boats, planes, travel, thrills, and the list goes on. When we fall for that lie, like the Israelites of old, we tend to make an idol of *things* and turn our backs on the only One who can eternally satisfy and fulfill our deepest longings.

WE SUFFER THE CONSEQUENCES

The trouble with making an idol of material things is that they are temporal. They are vulnerable, volatile, and will one day let us down. The market can crash, beauty fades, status can be lost, family and friends can betray us, and alarm systems can be compromised. Counting on penultimate things to answer ultimate questions never ends well. Thus, God's love is still tough. He allows us to experience the full slate of consequences for doing life as if he doesn't exist— disappointment, despair, brokenness, shame, guilt, regret, emptiness, loneliness, and—finally, death.

Don't lose sight of this, though. Just as in the day of the prophets, God's tough love is meant to be redemptive, not punitive. God lets us hit bottom so we will hopefully one day look up and turn to him. God is a practitioner of reality therapy. He lets our brushes with reality become the catalysts for the desire for a new reality—one with him in the picture of our lives.

GOD'S GOODNESS WINS US BACK

If you read the prophets with a jaundiced eye, you might conclude that God is like the evil prison warden whose primary leadership mantra is the ironic, "The beatings will continue until the morale improves." Because God cares for his people, he sent the prophets to warn them of the consequences of their unfaithfulness with the hope that they would return to him. When they refused to listen, God did not take delight in the consequences of their disobedience—his heart was broken. We could even say his love was a suffering love.

That is why God's message through the prophets began to turn a bit when he was suffering with his people in the midst of their travail. Through Hosea, God opines:

> Then I will win her back once again.
>   I will lead her into the desert
>   and speak tenderly to her there.
> I will return her vineyards to her
>   and transform the Valley of Trouble into a gateway of hope.[17]

Ultimately it will be the kindness and goodness of God that will lead Israel home. Hosea sums it up beautifully by saying that in the last days, when God is going to do his best redeeming work, "the people will return and devote themselves to the LORD their God and to David's descendant, their king. In the last days, they will tremble in awe of the LORD and of his goodness."[18]

As the next chapter unfolds you will see the fulfillment of this prophetic word and how God's goodness is going to lead people back to himself. In the meantime, to prepare your mind and spirit for what is next, set aside a few minutes to take an honest inventory of your life. Notate any hurt, habit, or hang-up that is diminishing the quality or value of your life. Trace it back to the source. Identify it. Seek to understand it—its power over you and in you. Then, think about what it would feel like if you were free from its clutches. Imagine the weight of regret and responsibility being lifted off your shoulders. Dream about being saved from your very worst self and discovering the secret to becoming your very best self…and you'll be ready to read and comprehend how God saves!

THE STORY BETWEEN THE STORY

As it turns out, God's chosen people are disobedient stinkers who have pretty much hit rock bottom. Their Promised Land is seized by foreign powers, Solomon's beautiful Temple is destroyed, and God's people are led away into exile. Among the Jews living in exile decades later are two great men named Ezra and Nehemiah. Ezra is a priest who leads a group of Israelites back to Jerusalem from Babylon, leads them in rebuilding the Temple, and leads them to repentance. Nehemiah returns from Persia to lead the people in rebuilding the city wall. Thanks to God's faithfulness through Ezra and Nehemiah, the children of Israel still remaining in exile now have a home to return to. But this good news is nothing compared to the great hope that God still has up his sleeve.

While many of the Jewish people do return to their homeland, the nation will never again return to the political prominence it enjoyed under its great kings. For centuries, God's people endure oppression under foreign rule by the Persians, then the Greeks, then the Romans. The Temple is desecrated and the prophets grow silent.

But deep in the hearts of the children of Israel, despite the silence, hope whispers. The people remember the prophecies of Isaiah and Jeremiah. They remember God's promises of deliverance through his Chosen One—a Messiah who would break the yoke of slavery. As centuries pass,

God's people begin to imagine their Messiah will be another David—a great military leader to break the oppression of their foreign overlords. But what they seem to miss is that so much of the prophecy points to a different kind of savior—one who would be despised and rejected. A man of sorrows, acquainted with deepest grief, and led like a lamb to slaughter. But what kind of Messiah is this?

After centuries of silence from God and oppression from foreign powers, God's people are desperately watching for something big to happen. And finally, it does. But it comes in such an altogether unexpected way that many of them miss it completely.

And that, in a nutshell, is the story between the story.

Jesus

UNDER FOREIGN RULE

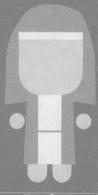

Persians

Greeks

Romans

6

GOD SAVES

God has come to save us! Hurray!

But before God can save us, he must become one of us. That miracle takes shape around 4 BC when a baby is born in Bethlehem. The angelic orders are: "Give him the name Jesus, because he will save his people from their sins."[1]

Herod the Great, Rome's puppet ruler over the region, tries to kill the infant. But God foils Herod, who turns out not to be as great as he thinks he is. Jesus grows up in a tight Jewish family in Nazareth, a small village in Galilee.

At about the age of thirty, Jesus goes public. He gets baptized in the Jordan River by his cousin John (a.k.a. John the Baptizer), then heads straight for the Judean wilderness to connect with God. While there, Satan tries to persuade Jesus to take a different road, but Jesus resists the temptations.

After setting up shop in the lake town of Capernaum, Jesus calls twelve locals to be his disciples. Over the next three years, the crowds celebrate Jesus, stand in awe of his miracles, and adore his teachings—but waffle on following him. They like his sizzle and style, but not his talk about suffering.

In early 30 AD, Jesus closes down shop in Galilee. He tells the disciples they're going to Jerusalem for Passover. When they approach the capital city, mob momentum grows as political fervor picks up. Someone finds a small donkey for Jesus to mount and ride into Jerusalem. The crowds go wild. They scream for him to be the One who will save them from Roman occupation.

During Passover week, Jesus spends several days in the Temple courtyards being assailed by his adversaries. They know that if the crowds crown him king, Caesar will crush Jerusalem. They won't let that happen. So gifted leaders from the world's most moral religion and the world's most powerful government conspire to kill the only good man who has ever lived. And they do. On a hill outside the city gates, on a Friday afternoon in April of 30 AD, Jesus gives up his life.

But on the third day, God surprises everyone by raising Jesus back to life. Jesus assures the twelve disciples that he's not a ghost and tells them to take this news everywhere. Fifty days later, Jesus returns to heaven to be with his Father. Mission accomplished.

GOD'S STORY

Before Jesus is born, it looks to the people of Israel like God is silent—or worse, absent. Is he ignoring them? Is he neglecting them? Has he forgotten them?

But God does not forget his promise—he just waits for the right time to make his move. And when it is time, he does.

"When the right time came, God sent his Son."[2]

God's sending of his Son is not generic—it is particular. He sends Jesus to a particular place, at a particular time, to a particular people. If we don't understand that place, that time, and those people, we can never understand Jesus. If God, in his infinite wisdom, decides to send his only Son to Jews living in Palestine some 2,000 years ago, then we must try to understand why.

That's why we turn to the Jewish Story first—so we can understand the Jesus Story.

THE JEWISH STORY[3]

Israel has always been a tiny nation. If it were part of the United States, it would be one of the smallest states—about the size of New Jersey or Vermont.

Size isn't necessarily a big deal, except that Israel in the time of Christ is located right in the middle of major superpowers like Egypt, Syria, Babylon (Iraq), and Persia (Iran). Like a political football, Israel is constantly kicked around by her big bully neighbors. Oppression is the norm.

When Jesus goes into Galilee "proclaiming the good news of God,"[4] his fellow Jews don't have much good news in their lives—and haven't for a long time. They have been under foreign domination for centuries. Under the Persians, Jews experience relative freedom. Under the Greeks, Jews face pressure to become Hellenistic, or Greek-like. Under the Romans, Jews are forced to endure police brutality perpetrated by professional Roman soldiers.

What would you do if you were facing hostile treatment every day from unwelcome overlords? Probably exactly what the oppressed Jews do. First, they learn to despise all non-Jews, a.k.a. Gentiles. Second, they develop a zealous hope for a deliverer, a Messiah, who will one day liberate them. Third, they seek to be faithful to God the best they can. Under Roman oppression, this faithfulness takes different forms.

Politics in Jesus's Day

Politics and religion are not separated in first-century Palestine like they are in twenty-first-century America. They go hand-in-hand. Jews relate faith and culture in several ways.

"Keep the peace" is the motto of the Sadducees. They will do anything to keep Rome off their backs, even if it means compromising their beliefs. They "go along to get along." They work within the system to keep the Empire happy, managing the priesthood and the Jewish Supreme Court (Sanhedrin) for maximum Jewish benefit. Their goal? To keep their fellow Jews in line, especially the rebellious ones up in Galilee who are always looking for a Messiah to crush Rome.

"No compromise" is the motto of the Pharisees. They are polar opposites to the Sadducees. Practicing strict obedience to the law of Moses, they are eager to show Rome how much different (and better) they are. So they observe kosher food laws, diligently honor the Sabbath, and regard Gentiles as worse than dogs. They are not given to violence, but they will not compromise their faith. Period.

"Take no prisoners" is the motto of the Zealots. This is the crowd that is always ready for a fight, prepared to die for a cause. They are the religious terrorists of Jesus's day. Hating Roman force, taxation, and idolatry, they believe that freedom is worth any price. And they are more than willing to pay it.

"Let's move to the desert" is the motto of the Essenes. They decide it is impossible to obey the law of Moses while under the thumb of pagan Romans. So they withdraw to the desert beyond the Dead Sea. There they start communes devoted to studying the Torah, praying, and living disciplined lives.

"Who's got time for politics?" is the question asked by average Jews. They're just trying to eke out a living. This describes 90 percent of Jews in Jesus's day— farmers, shepherds, day-laborers, and merchants. They have no time for politics. They must work for a living, feed their family, and obey God to the best of their ability.

But whatever their political stances, these Jews all have one thing in common: They want their freedom. They want God to fulfill his promise to Abraham and give them a land where they can prosper. They want God to send a new Moses to rescue them from oppression. They want God to raise up a new David who will defeat their enemies. They want God to send them a Messiah, a Deliverer, a King.

This is the world into which Jesus is born.

THE JESUS STORY

Anonymity

You would expect Jesus's birth to be a royal event involving royal people in a royal city. Instead, an unknown teenage Jewish girl named Mary learns from an angel that she's going to get pregnant through the power of God's Spirit. Her equally unknown fiancé, Joseph, is shocked when he hears the story but decides not to end the engagement. As the pregnancy nears term, the couple walks eighty miles to backwater Bethlehem, where they are ushered to a cattle stall for the delivery. Soon her water breaks, and baby Jesus is born and placed in a smelly animal feeding trough. The surprise of the event is captured in a Christmas carol: "How silently, how silently, the wondrous gift is given."[5] Indeed. Hardly anyone knows he is born.

Jesus remains a no-name during his childhood and early adulthood. He lives for three decades in Nazareth, an isolated town north of Jerusalem in Galilee. He learns carpentry and masonry from Joseph. In fact, he and Joseph may help build the nearby city of Sepphoris. Even so, only a handful of people know him as a boy or a young man. For his first thirty years on earth, he is simply unknown.

Popularity

Jesus steps onto center stage at about the age of thirty, launching his public ministry. It starts when his cousin John baptizes him in the Jordan River. Initially John resists, because his baptism is for people who want to change their ways from evil to good. And he knows Jesus doesn't need that. Yet Jesus persuades and John relents. Emerging from the water, Jesus is overjoyed to hear the voice of his Father in heaven saying, "You are my Son, whom I love; with you I am well pleased."[6] And the power of God's Spirit envelops him.

Shortly after his baptism, Jesus goes into the nearby Judean desert to pray for strength to take the road of redemptive suffering before him. But the evil one ambushes him and tries to talk him into taking the road of popularity, fame, and power. Jesus, listening to God's voice, resists.

Emerging unscathed from Satan's assault, Jesus goes from town to town in Galilee, stating his reason for coming to earth: to announce that God's Kingdom is available to all.

> Jesus went into Galilee, where he preached God's Good News.
> "The time promised by God has come at last!" he announced.
> "The Kingdom of God is near!"[7]

In other words, "You won't believe what God has in store for you. It's what you've been waiting for your whole life. It's so close you can touch it. In fact, he's looking at you right now."

As he travels around, Jesus not only offers God's Kingdom to all. He also invites people to follow him as he follows God.

> One day as Jesus was walking along the shore of the Sea of Galilee, he saw two brothers—Simon, also called Peter, and Andrew—throwing a net into the water, for they fished for a living. Jesus called out to them, "Come, follow me."[8]

Many accept his invitation, going with him wherever he goes. They learn from him. They apprentice themselves to him. They become his disciples.

People are finally taking notice of Jesus of Nazareth. For the next two years, his popularity soars. Almost everyone loves him. Why is he so admired? What makes people want to be with him?

Jesus's Miracles

What first catches people's attention is his miracles. Almost forty are listed in the four Gospels. Each one shows God's power. Each one meets a human need. Each one gives a glimpse of heaven on earth. But they come in different flavors.

Some miracles show Jesus's power over nature, like the time he is in a small boat with his disciples on the Sea of Galilee. It's late at night, a furious storm erupts, and everyone is scared spitless. Everyone except Jesus. He quietly silences the storm and calms the waves. [9] Mere child's play.

Some miracles demonstrate his authority over sickness, as when he heals a man with leprosy. Lepers in Jesus's day are considered contagious, off-limits from all social contact. Yet Jesus gladly touches the man to unveil the compassion of God and to preview a time in the future when sickness, disease, and death will be nothing but distant memories. [10]

Some miracles display his supremacy over evil, as when he casts a "legion" of demons out of a man who is as strong as an ox, as crazy as a loon, and as scary as a roaring lion. Yet Jesus walks straight up to him and exorcises his evil spirits. The sheer power of Jesus is seen in the moments that follow. The man, once tormented and naked, is now "sitting there fully clothed and perfectly sane." [11]

Some miracles reveal his power over the ultimate enemy, death, like the time a despondent father asks Jesus to save his dying daughter. Jesus calmly walks into the room of the girl, now expired, takes her by the hand and says, "Little girl, get up!" She does. Everyone's jaw drops as he presents her alive to her parents. [12]

Jesus's Teachings[13]

People also flock to Jesus because they are amazed at what comes out of his mouth. When he teaches, he doesn't give a list of dos and don'ts—he describes who God is and what life in his Kingdom is like. Sometimes Jesus gives crystal-clear moral principles that are universal, like "Do to others whatever you would like them to do to you. This is the essence of all that is taught in the law and the prophets."[14] He knows that life is more than rules—and that all the best rules have a golden thread running through them. That's why we call this the Golden Rule—it is invaluable in summarizing God's intent for human relationships.

But mostly Jesus speaks in colorful and memorable stories that first-century Palestinian peasants can understand. Called parables, these teachings often reveal the true God. Three of his most famous parables are found in Luke 15. In the first story, a sheep strays from the fold and keeps eating grass until it has accidentally nibbled its way to lostness. The shepherd leaves the ninety-nine safe sheep to find the one that is lost, then throws a party because he is so overjoyed and thankful.[15]

In the second story, a woman unintentionally lets a valuable coin slip between her fingers. It's lost. She turns the house upside down until she finds it. Then she invites friends and neighbors over for a celebration.[16]

The third story concerns a father and his two sons. Over the years, the youngest son has grown sick of his father and tired of the family rules. So he decides to leave home with his cut of the inheritance. After wasting it all on wine, women, and song, he's impoverished. Knowing that his father's servants eat better than he does, he decides to go home, apologize, and ask to work as a servant, not to be reinstated as a son. But to everyone's surprise, the father receives the son with merciful love, not with harsh judgment. And he throws a party that is heard for miles around. In the meantime, the older son is proud of his hard work and family loyalty. When he hears that his reckless brother has returned home to a hero's welcome, he blows a gasket. How dare the father show mercy to this black sheep in the family! Yet the father explains, "Look, dear son, you have always stayed by me, and everything I have is yours. We had to celebrate this happy day. For your brother was dead and has come back to life! He was lost, but now he is found!"[17]

In each of these stories the main character represents God. And the God and Father of Jesus Christ cares deeply about anyone who is lost from his purposes and love.

Jesus's Friendships

Finally, the common person loves Jesus because he offers them his friendship. When it comes to choosing friends, Jesus is inclusive, not exclusive.

When he chooses the twelve disciples, his most intimate circle of friends, whom does he include? A hotheaded political zealot, a hated tax collector, and some foul-smelling fishermen. Talk about diversity!

When he encounters women who are caught in adultery or trapped in prostitution, what does he do? He forgives them.

When he meets despised neighbors who are considered "sinners," how does he treat them? He eats meals with them. He enjoys being called a "friend of sinners."

When he runs into "unclean" people whom everyone avoids like the plague, how does he respond? He allows a woman who is hemorrhaging to touch his robe. He touches and heals lepers whose faces and fingers are rotting off.

Jesus accepts everyone, even (maybe especially) those who are considered to be "far from God."

Rejection

At the peak of his popularity, Jesus begins to hear rumblings of rejection.

Not everyone likes his miracles. After Jesus raises his good friend Lazarus from the dead, the Pharisees and Sadducees fear his actions will incite other Galileans to rebel against Rome. So they decide to kill him.

Not everyone likes his teachings either. When Jesus claims to have authority and power to forgive sins, the Pharisees and Sadducees accuse him of blasphemy and decide to take him out.

And not everyone likes his choice of friends. Every time he shares a meal with the irreligious and immoral, he moves more directly into the crosshairs of the Jewish leaders.

During his last six months, Jesus knows the religious powerbrokers want to end his life. He knows their plans, yet he trusts God for his future. So in the spring of 30 AD, he heads to Jerusalem for the final showdown.

His Last Week

During his final week, each day is significant.[18]

On Sunday, he enters the capital city on a donkey, with crowds singing and shouting, "Hosanna to the Son of David" meaning "You're our king! You're our new David! You're the one who can save us from our enemies!"

On Monday he heads for the Temple. When he arrives, he is incensed to see merchants selling sacrificial animals at sky-high prices to make a profit on worshippers. He confronts them:

"It is written...'My house will be called a house of prayer,' but you are making it a 'den of robbers.'"[19]

Then he overturns their sales stalls in righteous anger. The Jewish leaders, believing he has judged the holy Temple, vow to kill him.

On Tuesday he teaches in the Temple courtyards all day. It starts with the religious leaders engaging him in a game of "Stump the Rabbi." He answers all their tough questions, asks them tougher questions, and simply ties them in knots. He also calls out the experts in the law of Moses for their hypocrisy—saying one thing and doing another. They are not appreciative, to say the least.

On Wednesday, we don't know what Jesus does. We assume he spends the day in quiet rest with his friends in nearby Bethany.

On Thursday, Jesus hosts a Passover meal for his disciples that evening. He ends the meal by telling the Twelve that he is about to die, as the Passover Lamb of God, on their behalf. After dinner, he leads his inner circle into a nearby olive grove to pray for clarity and to surrender his will, again, to God. As the night gets darker and darker, one of his disciples betrays Jesus to his opponents. They arrest him and lead him off to be tried on trumped-up charges in two kangaroo courts, one Jewish and one Roman. All along the way he is brutally beaten and mercilessly mocked.

On Friday, the Roman governor Pilate yields to the demands of the religious leaders and sentences Jesus to death by crucifixion. Roman soldiers lead Jesus outside Jerusalem to a hill that looks like a skull, and there they crucify him. They nail him to a cross at 9:00 a.m., where he hangs for six hours, mostly silent. But the few words he speaks reveal who he really is.

His Last Words

Here are his seven statements from the cross.

- "Father, forgive them, for they don't know what they are doing."[20]

- "I assure you, today you will be with me in paradise."[21]

- "When Jesus saw his mother standing there beside the disciple he loved, he said to her, 'Dear woman, here is your son.' And he said to this disciple, 'Here is your mother.' And from then on, this disciple took her into his home."[22]

- "Eloi, Eloi, lema sabachthani?" which means "My God, my God, why have you abandoned me?"[23]

- "Jesus knew that his mission was now finished, and to fulfill Scripture he said, 'I am thirsty.'"[24]

- [Jesus said], "It is finished!"[25]

- "Then Jesus shouted, 'Father, I entrust my spirit into your hands!' And with those words he breathed his last."[26]

"And with those words he breathed his last." Jesus is finally dead. He is buried quietly and without fanfare on a Friday afternoon before sunset.

The Great Reversal

But on Sunday morning God raises him back to life! We call it the resurrection. It is God's stamp of approval that Jesus is God's Son. It shows that love is stronger than evil and death. It proves once and for all that God is love.

That's the Jesus story. If it's the greatest story ever told, that's because it tells the story of the greatest life ever lived.

How does your story fit into the Jesus story? First, he gave you a pattern to follow. While it's easy to remember that Jesus is divine, don't forget that he is also human. Like all humans, he had to deal with being anonymous, popular, and even rejected. Here's what we can learn from him as we face each experience.

FACING ANONYMITY

Everyone hungers for significance. Being made in God's image, we long for eternal joy and celebration. So it's only natural that if we find ourselves in a season where we feel unnoticed and unknown, we tend to feel lost and lonely. Rather than lash out in anger or sink into despair, this is the time to do two things. First, ask God to help you become acquainted with someone who can become your friend. Someone who will see you, hear you, know you, and value you—and vice versa. One good friend can ease, maybe even erase, the burden of anonymity.

Second, draw close to God. Take time every day to read the Bible, especially the Psalms. Set aside a place to pour out your heart in prayer. Be honest when you talk to your heavenly Father. He knows what you're thinking and how you're feeling, so you won't surprise him. Rejoice in the discovery that God knows you. Learn to let that suffice for now.

FACING POPULARITY

Few things are as heady or addicting as being liked. It's far more fun to be popular than to feel anonymous. But popularity has its shadow-side. It can suck us into people pleasing. Soon we weigh every move based on crowd applause.

When that happens, remember how Jesus handled his popularity: He lived his life before an audience of One. You can choose to do the same. Seek the applause of God only. If others clap for you, that's fine. But beware of bowing to the crowds. They are fickle. They can just as easily crown you as crucify you.

FACING REJECTION

Nobody handles rejection better than Jesus. He doesn't defend himself against his enemies, and he doesn't retaliate. He simply leans into his heavenly Father and has confidence that love will see him through. He is not some fatalist. He is a clear-eyed realist. Faith in God gives him the vision and strength to take each step, especially during his final week. He knows enough about God to know that resurrection follows death.

Following Jesus means we live for him and live like him. When we face rejection, we do what Jesus has done. We tell God what we are feeling, we ask for what we hope he will do, and then we proclaim, "Yet I want your will to be done, not mine." [27] And the whole time, we trust that God can transform death into new life. This is the only way to face rejection and not be ultimately defeated.

JESUS HAS COME TO SAVE YOU

But Jesus doesn't just give you a pattern for living. He has come to save you. Behind this idea are five truths that can be anchor points for your life.

God Has Created You

Your father and mother are cocreators, but behind it all is God. That makes him your Maker. He wanted and willed your existence.

God Knows You

He knows the good and rejoices in it. He knows the bad and the ugly. He sees how the bad and the ugly are damaging you, others, and his reputation. That's not his vision for your life.

God Loves You, Just as You Are

If he didn't, how could he love you at all? You are always just as you are. And that's the you God loves. As Dallas Willard has said so eloquently: "We must understand that God does not love us without liking us—through gritted teeth—as Christian love is sometimes thought to do. Rather, out of the eternal freshness of his perpetually self-renewed being, the heavenly Father cherishes the earth and each human being upon it. The fondness, the endearment, the unstintingly affectionate regard of God toward all his creatures is the natural outflow of what he is to the core—which we vainly try to capture with our tired but indispensable old word love."[28]

God Wants to Save You

Why does God want to save you? So that you can experience his love. So that you can live with him and enjoy him now. So that you can live with him and enjoy him forever.

God Loves You So Much...

God loves you so much that he has sent his Son, Jesus, to be born for you, to live for you, to die for you, to be raised for you. He has sent Jesus to save you.

How Exactly Does Jesus Save You?

He saves you by taking your place. "Christ died for us" is one of the most common New Testament descriptions of why Jesus died.[29] We deserve his death, but he dies so we won't have to die. He takes our place on the cross, in death, and in judgment. As a result, we go free. We are saved from the guilt and shame of sin. We are saved from the futility of an empty life. We are saved from the demon of narcissism. We are saved from the evil of arrogance. We are saved from ourselves. Jesus saves us from all that is not of God.

Jesus saves! Hallelujah!

THE STORY BETWEEN THE STORY

Jesus is alive, death is defeated, and it's time for the victory tour! Jesus appears to the women at his tomb, then to his disciples, then to lots of other people—there was even a time when he appeared to over 500 at once. A bunch of people see the risen Jesus with their own eyes, which is a big reason the Gospel doesn't die out after Jesus's very public crucifixion. Jesus is back, and the disciples are pumped! But after forty days, he tells them the Holy Spirit is coming to help them, and then goes up to heaven right before their eyes.

Not long after this, the disciples are gathered together in Jerusalem when a rushing wind blows through the room. It's the Holy Spirit filling each of them with himself…and with the ability to speak a different language. This comes in handy when they go outside and find a crowd made up of Jews from all over the world who—you guessed it—speak a bunch of other languages. Peter preaches, Jews from all over the world are saved, and 3,000 new believers are baptized (and they only counted the men)!

The church in Judea and Samaria grows like crazy, and the Pharisees are none too pleased. One of them, Saul, is a real go-getter, and is determined to stop these crazy Jesus-followers even if it means killing them. He gets permission to take a road trip to Damascus and drag any believers he finds back to Jerusalem in chains. On the road, a blinding light stops Saul in his tracks, and a voice asks, "Saul, why are you persecuting me?" It's Jesus (*awkward!*), and Saul doesn't really have a good answer for him. After a personal encounter with the risen Jesus and a three-day time-out in Damascus, Saul's sight is restored and he switches sides, becoming the ultimate go-getter *for* the Gospel. After meeting Jesus, he's a completely different person. Saul even started using his Greek name, Paul.

And that, in a nutshell, is the story between the story.

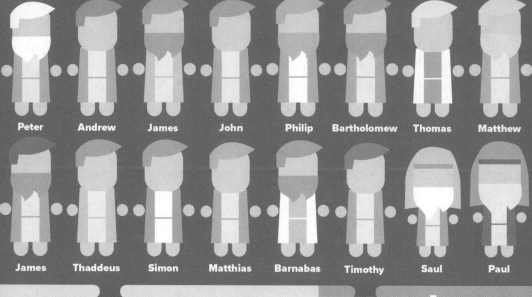

Peter · Andrew · James · John · Philip · Bartholomew · Thomas · Matthew

James · Thaddeus · Simon · Matthias · Barnabas · Timothy · Saul · Paul

Pharisees

THE HOLY SPIRIT IS COMING TO HELP

I'LL BE BACK

Jesus

GOD SENDS

After Jesus's crucifixion and resurrection, his story begins to spread. Through the boldness of his followers, the Good News permeates the city of Jerusalem, the region of Judea, and the not-so-friendly neighboring Samaria.

But for the Gospel to travel to the ends of the earth, God needs someone very special for the job. So he chooses…Saul of Tarsus? The fanatic who hates Christians? The tenacious terrorist who arrests anyone connected to the church? The man of zeal whose mission is to rid Judaism of those who think Jesus is the Messiah?

God is either a poor judge of character, or he has a great sense of humor, or he simply works with what's available. Whatever the reason, Saul is God's man.

After his conversion, Saul learns all he can about Jesus. He studies and prays in the desert, poring over the Hebrew Scriptures in search of promises about the

Messiah. One day he gets a clear message straight from God: He and his mentor, Barnabas, are to be the first missionaries.

So together they travel west to Cyprus, then north into Asia Minor, which today we call Turkey. Their message receives mixed reviews: Some love it, some hate it, some need more time to think about it. After several months on the road, experiencing more than their fair share of rejections and beatings, they return to Antioch to give a report to the church.

Within a year, Paul again heads for parts unknown, this time partnering with Silas instead of Barnabas. Halfway into the trip, God reveals to him that their destination is Europe—specifically Macedonia and Greece. They plant churches in major population centers like Philippi, Athens, and Corinth. On the way back to Antioch, Paul stops in Ephesus and starts a new church there. Once again the reception is mixed: Some believe the message, some don't, some decide to make trouble.

The troublemakers eventually arrest Paul in Jerusalem, hell-bent on killing him. He appeals to his rights as a Roman citizen, thereby saving his skin and receiving permission to plead his case before Roman authorities. Imprisoned first in Caesarea, then eventually in Rome, Paul defends his faith, tells the Jesus story, and invites all listeners to believe. Some do, some don't. God uses those who do believe to spread the Good News throughout the known world. The Gospel finally is going to the ends of the earth, through a most surprising man.

GOD'S STORY

As you know, Jesus is the climax of God's Great Story. His life, death, and resurrection are Good News for the whole world. But only a handful of people in a tiny corner of the world know about it initially. How does the message gain traction and go global?

JESUS'S MARCHING ORDERS

Before he goes back to heaven, Jesus gives marching orders to his followers:

> You will receive power when the Holy Spirit comes upon you. And you will be my witnesses, telling people about me everywhere—in Jerusalem, throughout Judea, in Samaria, and to the ends of the earth.[1]

The book of Acts records how God's Spirit sends out the first Christians to fulfill this command in a specific geographical order: Jerusalem, Judea, Samaria, and the ends of earth.

It all begins fifty days after the resurrection, when Simon Peter lives up to his name ("Rocky") by boldly telling the Jesus story to a huge crowd gathered in Jerusalem at the feast of Pentecost. Three thousand are saved and baptized. As Peter continues proclaiming this Good News, the reception gets icy. He and John are arrested, beaten, and ordered to keep quiet. They don't. And the word keeps spreading in the Holy City.

A few years later, Stephen tells the Jesus story to a packed-out synagogue in Jerusalem. His reward? He is arraigned before the Jewish Supreme Court, judged as a heretic, and stoned to death. His martyrdom leads to a city-wide persecution of Jesus-followers, most of whom flee Jerusalem for the hills of Judea and Samaria.

Once in Samaria, Philip tells some locals about Jesus, and they cross the line of faith. He then tells a North African court official about Jesus, and he too believes and is baptized. Soon Peter goes into uncharted territory by telling Cornelius, a Roman military officer and God-fearing Gentile, that he can be saved through Christ as well. And he is, along with his whole household. The Good News is permeating Judea and Samaria. Now there's just one more step. And it's a big one.

Enter Saul of Tarsus, who will eventually become Paul the apostle.

FROM SAUL OF TARSUS TO PAUL THE APOSTLE

Paul's story consumes over half of the book of Acts. Other than Jesus, he is the most influential and important person in the New Testament. His story unfolds in three key parts.

Saul Without Jesus

Saul is born about the same time as Jesus, in southeast Turkey. As a Roman citizen, he has legal rights that will come in handy and save his life more than once. His parents raise him as a strict Jew and name him after Israel's first king. His father is a Pharisee, and Saul himself will follow in those footsteps as an adult. Saul's white-hot zeal to protect the purity of Judaism leads him to fight against an emerging group of his kinsmen who say Jesus is Lord and Messiah. He becomes "public enemy number one" of the churches.

To get an idea of what Saul is like prior to meeting Jesus, here are two descriptions. First we see him through the eyes of Luke, the author of Acts.

> The Jewish leaders were infuriated by Stephen's accusation, and they shook their fists at him in rage...They rushed at him and dragged him out of the city and began to stone him. His accusers took off their coats and laid them at the feet of a young man named Saul. [And] they stoned him...[and] he died. Saul was one of the witnesses, and he agreed completely with the killing of Stephen.[2]

And here is how Saul sees himself:

> For you have heard of my previous way of life in Judaism, how intensely I persecuted the church of God and tried to destroy it.[3]

This is Saul—a fervent zealot who believes God has called him to destroy the church. But his life is about to be turned upside down.

Saul Meets Jesus

When the same story is repeated over and over in a book, you take notice. Saul's story of meeting Jesus is so significant that it's told three times in Acts. Here are the highlights.[4]

Saul is a one-man wrecking machine.

His goal? To wipe out the "Messiah-Jesus" movement.

His method? To travel to synagogues, arrest Christ-followers, and bring them before the Jewish Supreme Court, where they must recant or die.

His conversion? One day while traveling to Damascus to arrest Jesus-followers, he is struck down by a heavenly light. While lying in the dirt he hears a voice that thunders, "Saul! Why are you harassing me?" Clueless, Saul asks, "Who's talking to me?" The voice answers, "I am Jesus. I'm the one you're persecuting. Now go on into Damascus and wait for me to contact you."

His new calling? Blinded by the light, Saul stumbles into Damascus and waits for three days. God finally sends Ananias, a Jesus-follower, to go to Saul with this message: "God has chosen you to take the Jesus story far and wide—to Jews whom you love and to non-Jews whom you don't yet love. And along the way, you will suffer more than you can imagine."

This is the turning point for Saul. He changes teams, changes loyalties, changes his scorecard.

Paul with Jesus

Following the Damascus Road experience, Saul does not go straight to a travel agent and plan a mission trip. Instead, he goes into the desert for a decade to study Scripture and seek divine direction.

The direction comes in a vision God gives to the rapidly growing church in Antioch, the first great sending church in history.

> Among the prophets and teachers of the church at Antioch of
> Syria were Barnabas, Simeon...Lucius...Manaen...and Saul. One
> day as these men were worshiping the Lord and fasting, the

> Holy Spirit said, "Appoint Barnabas and Saul for the special work to which I have called them." So after more fasting and prayer, the men laid their hands on them and sent them on their way. So Barnabas and Saul were sent out by the Holy Spirit.[5]

Thus begins Paul's new role as Jesus's ambassador to the world. Over the next decade he leads three massive mission trips to take the Gospel message to the known world.

First Mission Trip[6]

When he goes on his first trip in the late AD 40s, Paul takes two companions: Barnabas and Mark. Barnabas is the leading apostle at the church in Antioch, and Mark is his younger cousin. They set out for Cyprus, Barnabas's home, then head north to Galatia.

Plan A is to take the message of Jesus to Jews who typically gather in synagogues on the Sabbath. Since Jews are looking for the Messiah, perhaps they will be open to the idea that Jesus fits the bill. If the Jews receive the message, great. If they reject it, there is still Plan B: Go to the Gentiles. It is on this first mission trip that Paul first experiences what God predicted through Ananias: serious persecution. He is even stoned in Lystra—but as everyone knows, you can't keep a good man down. The results of this first trip are impressive: Many Jews and non-Jews come to faith in Christ, and several churches are planted.

Second Mission Trip[7]

As Paul and Barnabas are planning their second journey, they get into a heated argument about whether or not Mark should accompany them. Barnabas says yes—he's family. Paul says no—he deserted us last time. They can't mend fences, so they go opposite directions. Paul takes two new travel partners on the second mission trip, Silas and Timothy, and they set sail in the early 50s.

After returning to the churches that they planted on the first trip, they angle northwest into Asia Minor and eventually, thanks to a divine vision, into Europe. Their strategy is to focus on major cities in Greece and stay in each one as long as possible. Paul is arrested in, or forcibly kicked out of, almost every city he enters. His opponents? Jews who are still angry at him from his first trip. But he does manage to stay eighteen months in Corinth, where he sees remarkable results. He also writes letters to several of the churches he has planted. Once more, many people come to faith in Jesus, and many new churches are started.

Third Mission Trip[8]

In the mid-50s, Paul circles back to the churches he has planted on trips one and two, before settling down in Ephesus for twenty-four months. Again he writes letters to churches, surely having no idea that one day these letters would be considered the church's Scripture.

Arrest, Trial, Release

After a huge riot in Ephesus forced him to flee for his life, Paul receives a surprising vision from God. Next stop? Jerusalem. You mean the place where they crucified Jesus? And stoned Stephen to death? Same place. Yet Paul is not afraid.

> And now I am bound by the Spirit to go to Jerusalem. I don't
> know what awaits me, except that the Holy Spirit tells me
> in city after city that jail and suffering lie ahead. But my life

is worth nothing to me unless I use it for finishing the work
assigned me by the Lord Jesus—the work of telling others the
Good News about the wonderful grace of God.[9]

So Paul sails to Jerusalem. He is there less than a week when he is tracked down by a mob of angry Jews who drag him out of the Temple and manage to have him arrested and jailed. Standing before the Sanhedrin, he boldly tells about his conversion to Christ, which causes another riot. He is re-jailed.

When the Roman officer in charge hears that forty Jewish assassins have made an oath to kill Paul before they eat another meal, he smuggles Paul out of Jerusalem by night and removes him to Caesarea. Five hundred soldiers are called into action to protect a scrawny old rabbi.

At Caesarea he is locked away in prison for two years. Yet in the providence of God he is able to argue his case before two Roman governors—although neither is converted to faith in Christ. Not finding anything in Paul's conduct contrary to Roman law, they conclude that he should return to Jerusalem and face trial before the Sanhedrin. Paul refuses. He knows that if he does that, it will be his death sentence. So he invokes his rights as a Roman citizen and asks for a trial before Nero in Rome. The governors grant his request.

In the fall of AD 60, Paul sails to Rome—not as a free missionary, but as a prisoner awaiting trial. For two years he waits, under house arrest. Eventually he's acquitted and released. Then for five more years he travels westward, possibly as far as Spain. We don't know how far he actually goes. But we do know that he is arrested again, is sent to jail in Rome again, goes to trial again, and this time is found guilty. Tradition tells us he is beheaded outside of Rome in the mid-60s.

So ends the life of the most influential Christian and missionary in the history of the church. What does his life have to do with your life?

GOD CHOOSES SURPRISING PEOPLE

As we learned in chapter 4, God often chooses surprising people—David comes to mind. Paul is just as unexpected. So are Mac and Mary Owen.[10]

Mac and Mary grew up in church, met in high school, began dating, then brought a baby into the world before they were eighteen. Reluctantly they gave him up for adoption because they knew they couldn't care for him. Eventually they got married. But instead of settling down, they partied hard for several years. Mac started with alcohol, then graduated to heroin and finally to meth. Along the way they had two daughters, but the girls didn't know their daddy's addictions. Mac was masterful at hiding his habits. Meanwhile, Mary just kept looking the other way.

Early on a Sunday morning, one of his daughters woke up Mac and said, "Daddy, get up and go to church with us!" He didn't. But when he sobered up that afternoon, he had an unexpected come-to-Jesus experience that caused him to go to church that night. The Spirit of God so moved his heart that as the service ended, he stood before the congregation and told them of his failures and need for prayer. To his great surprise, they accepted him. Some even said, "You're our first drug addict!"

Mac started to attend rehab meetings, and in time kicked his destructive habits. He and Mary started a recovery ministry at their church, which allowed them to serve people whose problems they understood firsthand. Ten years later they heard about a national Christ-centered program called Celebrate Recovery (CR). Quickly they helped transition their church's recovery ministry into a CR ministry. Their story and gifts eventually led them to become leaders of CR at a national level.

God has used Mac and Mary to help thousands of people deal with their hurts, habits, and hang-ups. If God can choose Mac and Mary Owen to change the world, God can choose you.

GOD SENDS PEOPLE TO SURPRISING PLACES

Have you seen Dr. Seuss's classic sendoff book, *Oh the Places You'll Go?*[11] It describes some of the surprising sites you may one day see as you go through life. But even Dr. Seuss might be surprised to learn of the unexpected places God sends those who are ready to serve him.

I (Paul) have a close relative named Chris Harmon. His mom is my first cousin, which makes him my daughters' second cousin. (I think that makes him my first cousin once removed, but I wouldn't bet on it.) Although Chris and I didn't meet until we were both adults, we became friends immediately. He is a successful dermatologist. He and his wife, Sandy, have raised two beautiful and Christ-centered daughters. In the world's eyes, there's little more for them to accomplish. Yet he and Sandy had a sneaking suspicion that God created them for more than just work and family.

One day God gave them a vision of using Chris's medical skills to serve under-resourced people outside the United States. They began going on medical mission trips to Venezuela and Bolivia, serving the poorest of the poor. Then they sensed God calling them to do the same along the Amazon River in Brazil. There's no telling how many other countries they have gone to as ambassadors of Jesus. God has used them as envoys of grace to people-groups living in nations they never thought of going to when they were a young married couple. But God had different plans.

God loves to send people to surprising places. If God can send Chris and Sandy Harmon throughout South America, God can send you.

GOD USES PEOPLE TO DO SURPRISINGLY GREAT THINGS FOR HIM

When we think of people who have left an indelible imprint on the world, we tend to think of them during their heyday, when everyone knew they were great. It's hard to realize that they weren't always like that. We forget that they had ordinary childhoods, often ordinary adulthoods, before they ever did anything considered great. Here are some examples.

Mother Teresa

Before becoming known worldwide as the face of compassion, Mother Teresa was Mary Teresa Bojaxhiu, an unknown girl from Macedonia with Albanian roots raised in a Roman Catholic family. She taught in India for seventeen years, then felt called by God to serve the underside of society in the streets of Calcutta. In time she was recognized for her work, receiving the Nobel Prize for Peace in 1979 and being canonized in 2016, less than twenty years after her death. As a humanitarian of the highest order, this little Albanian nun organized thousands of sisters to serve millions of sick and poor people in the name of Christ.[12] She did something surprisingly great for God.

Francis Collins

Francis Collins is best known as former Director of the National Institute of Health and Director of the Human Genome Project Research. With those two feathers in his cap, along with a PhD and MD, it might seem like he was always destined for greatness. But nobody in rural Virginia knew that when they were watching him grow up on a small farm where he helped his father raise cows and sheep. Eventually he made it into the Ivy League world and began to shine when he discovered a passion to help others through the study of genetics. His team at the Human Genome Project has identified the gene for cystic fibrosis and Huntington's Disease. Along the way he gave his life to Jesus Christ as his Lord and Savior, dedicating all his healing work to the glory of God. He is doing something surprisingly great for God.[13]

Dallas Willard

Born in rural Missouri during the Depression, Dallas Willard was anything but a future world-changer. After his mother's premature death when he was young, he was passed around from family member to family member during his growing-up years. He went to a small fundamentalist college to become a teacher and earned his teaching certificate. He was exposed to the world of philosophy at Baylor University, then completed his doctorate in philosophy. When he was hired by the University of Southern California, he had no idea that he would teach philosophy there for 47 years.[14] When he was asked to preach and teach Bible studies in SoCal churches, he didn't know that those notes would one day become the basis of modern devotional classics like *The Spirit of the Disciplines*, *The Divine Conspiracy*, and *Life Without Lack*. Dallas loved God, loved teaching students, and loved making discipleship accessible to anyone. He did something surprisingly great for God.

ARE YOU READY TO BE SENT?

It would be easy to think that since Jesus is the climax of God's Great Story, all we need to do now is wait for this world to end and heaven to begin. But that kind of thinking would be wrong.

We do not live in the time of waiting. We live in the time of sending. For 2,000 years now, Christians have been living in just such a time. It's the era of divine history in which God's Spirit is sending out his people to tell the Jesus story in all parts of the world.

You have the privilege of being alive during this time of sending.

Are you ready?

THE STORY BETWEEN THE STORY

The early church spreads like wildfire, thanks to the blessing of the Holy Spirit. While God is sending the apostles to preach the Gospel throughout the known world, they're also writing some very important letters. These letters help encourage followers of Jesus, instruct them in truth, and correct false teaching. And what's really cool is that those same letters continue to speak to all of us today through the New Testament.

Unfortunately, not everybody is stoked to hear the Good News of Jesus, and the apostles also have to put up with some heavy persecution. It seems wherever they carry news about Jesus, they encounter both blessing (as some people receive the Gospel) and opposition (as others reject it). The Roman emperor at this time, Nero, is a seriously bad dude who basically kills Christians for fun. And one of his successors, Domitian, isn't much of an improvement. Along with lots of other Christians, the apostles are tortured and eventually killed for their testimony about the risen Jesus. One by one, all of them are martyred. That is, all except one. The apostle named John, the Beloved Disciple who had been one of the original twelve, is tortured by Domitian, then exiled to the Island of Patmos.

It was a very difficult time for followers of Jesus to hold on to their faith. But just as they began to feel that they were being overwhelmed by persecution, God sent them some special encouragement through John and his visionary letter called Revelation, telling them to hang on, because God is going to win in the end!

And that, in a nutshell, is the story between the story.

Nero   **Domitian**

The Apostles

Island of Patmos

Hang on because God is going to win in the end!

GOD WINS

The number of stories in human history that have been lived and told is inestimable. The ones worth retelling and the ones that are enduring have one thing in common—a good ending. Have you ever sat through a three-hour movie and when the ending finally played out it was terrible? Moviegoers' responses are pretty universal, "You're kidding me! That's it?" We can't believe we spent all that time and invested all that emotional energy in a story that has an ending that isn't commensurate with the substance and significance of the plotlines that led us to the cusp of the climax.

What makes an ending less than satisfying? Well, some screenwriters go overboard attempting to explain everything by pointing out why things happened the way they did. In this way a screenplay is like a bad joke. If you have to explain it, it's usually not very funny. Or, in this case, it's not an engaging story. Sometimes it feels like the writer just runs out of steam and settles for a lame finale hoping the audience won't notice. We notice. The ending is not worthy of the weight of the story. Some endings are so convoluted and enigmatic that you can't figure out what really happened. When the credits roll you go, "Huh, what just happened?"

So, what makes for a good ending? The best endings don't always have to be happy. They just have to leave us with a sense of emotional satisfaction. What does that take? For most, it takes one of two things—resolution and/or redemption. Resolution is as simple as tying up all the loose ends. A mystery is solved. Quests are accomplished. Relationships are restored. Loose ends left untied in a story are as dissonant to our hearts as an unresolved dominant seventh chord is to the ear of a musician. Sam Gamgee says it well in *The Return of the King*: "I shan't call it the end, till we've cleared up the mess."[1]

Redemption occurs when something is learned, something of great value is gained, or someone is changed. In the Disney hit *Frozen*, Anna saves her sister's life by putting herself between Elsa and certain death. This act of true love transforms Elsa into the person she was meant to be. Even though moviegoers may have left the theater singing "Let It Go," it's Elsa's redemption that makes the ending emotionally gratifying.

You don't have to have both resolution and redemption for a satisfying ending. You can resolve all the tension in a comedy or an action movie and have a good laugh or experience a thrill without much redemption happening at all. Likewise, you can have a story that leaves some plotlines a mystery, but if redemption rules the day, all loose ends will soon be forgotten.

The best endings, though, have both. This is what makes *Les Misérables* such an enduring classic. It is the story of Jean Valjean, a convict hardened by a gross injustice, who finds grace from a Catholic priest, and it changes his life. In the final scene, Valjean is dying as Cossette (his adopted daughter) and her husband Marius (whose life he had saved during the Paris Uprising of 1832) comfort him. They are joined by the spiritual presence of Fantine (Cossette's mother), Eponine (a young woman who died in the uprising with an unrequited love for Marius), and the bishop who had shown Valjean mercy. As he dies, he is led into heaven by the bishop, Fantine, and Eponine as they sing together a moving chorus resolving the story and celebrating their redemption.

It's a powerful ending. It's not a happy ending, but it is deeply satisfying.

Which brings us to the end of God's Great Story. You have read how God creates, blesses, rescues, chooses, warns, saves, and sends his people. And now, the ending of this enduring story—God wins! It's not a lame ending. It is worthy of the weight and breadth of the story.

And, it is deeply satisfying for all things are resolved and redemption has the final word.

In the end, God wins, and it changes everything!

GOD'S
STORY

IN THE END, GOD WINS!

Three of the four Gospel writers record Jesus revealing to his disciples that one day he will return and put a wrap on history.[2] Paul tells us that in a moment, in the blink of an eye, the trumpet will sound and the end will come.[3] But the playbill for the final act is the Revelation of John, written near the end of the first century AD. In it, John, exiled to the island of Patmos, identifies the cast and foreshadows the plot of the final scene in God's Great Story. Revelation is a Tolkien-like drama with figurative language, encoded meanings, and a eucatastrophe, which is a sudden turn of events that gives hope to the hopeless. It is the turn that pierces us with joy and brings us to tears because we get a glimpse of the final victory![4]

It Is a Come-from-Behind Victory

The Roman emperor Nero martyred Peter and Paul near the end of his reign, sometime around AD 64–68. If that were not enough, he impaled Christians, covered them with pitch, and lit them for use as pathway lights on Roman roads. Domitian, who ruled Rome from AD 90–95, executed members of his own family who were suspected of being followers of Jesus. John, the last living disciple of the original twelve, is persecuted by Domitian and exiled to Patmos. Times were tough! The big issue was the conflict between Roman emperors demanding that people bow to them as their lord, and Christianity's devotion to the lordship of Christ. When confronted with this choice, many believers refused to kowtow to the Caesar and declared that Jesus is Lord. Needless to say, it did not end well for those who did. John refers to this tragic reality covertly in his revelation when he writes:

> I saw a woman sitting on a scarlet beast...The woman wore purple and scarlet clothing and beautiful jewelry made of gold and precious gems and pearls. In her hand she held a gold goblet full of obscenities and the impurities of her immorality. A mysterious name was written on her forehead: "Babylon the

Great, Mother of All Prostitutes and Obscenities in the World."
I could see that she was drunk—drunk with the blood of God's
holy people who were witnesses for Jesus. I stared at her in
complete amazement.[5]

Spiritually speaking it was Christians 0, Rome 42, and it was just the first quarter. The visiting team was in danger of having their spirits broken. One could feel the discouragement and hopelessness seeping in. So God sent the angel to give John an apocalyptic message—it's tough now, things don't look good, but hold on, God will win in the end!

It Features an Unlikely Hero

John is taken into heaven, and he sees the throne room. The throne, surrounded by twenty-four elders, represents the people of God from both Testaments. The Lord has a scroll in his right hand, but no one can break the seal on the scroll so that the contents may be read. John recounts:

Then I began to weep bitterly because no one was found
worthy to open the scroll and read it. But one of the twenty-
four elders said to me, "Stop weeping! Look, the Lion of the
tribe of Judah, the heir to David's throne, has won the victory.
He is worthy to open the scroll and its seven seals."
        Then I saw a Lamb that looked as if it had been slaught-
ered, but it was now standing between the throne and the four
living beings and among the twenty-four elders...And when
he took the scroll, the four living beings and the twenty-four
elders fell down before the Lamb... And they sang a new song
with these words:

"You are worthy to take the scroll
  and break its seals and open it.
For you were slaughtered, and your blood has ransomed
    people for God
  from every tribe and language and people and nation.
And you have caused them to become
  a Kingdom of priests for our God.
  And they will reign on the earth."[6]

The Lion of Judah is a Lamb. An unlikely hero for sure. How does a sacrificial lamb defeat the powers of the evil one and his minions? Our first inclination is that God is going to outslug the devil, overpower him with violent strength. But God knows that power can control evil, but it cannot ultimately vanquish it. Look around at human history…the violent use of power, even genocide, only creates seeds for more violence in the hearts of the vanquished, and they always sprout again. It generates an endless cycle—just look at Croats and Serbs, Hutus and Tutsis, Israelis and Palestinians.

Think of what the Lamb does as spiritual "rope-a-dope." Rope-a-dope is associated with Muhammad Ali in his 1974 Rumble in the Jungle with George Foreman. It's a strategy in which one fighter purposely puts himself in what appears to be a losing position, allowing his opponent to punch himself out to the point he becomes defenseless. Jesus allowed himself to be beaten, whipped, and nailed to the cross. Satan delivers every blow he can to defeat God's ultimate plan for saving and rescuing humanity. But love, perfect love, sacrificial love is impervious to hatred, force, and violence. Jesus did not answer his accusers, or mock his executioners, or call 10,000 angels. Instead, he calls out to his Father from the cross, "Forgive them, for they don't know what they are doing."[7]

Satan, at the end of the day, has punched himself out. The Lord Almighty just breathes on him and he falls to his eternal demise. As the apostle Paul declares, "Then the man of lawlessness will be revealed, but the Lord Jesus will slay him with the breath of his mouth and destroy him by the splendor of his coming."[8]

The Score Is Settled

One of the great challenges Christianity has faced through the centuries is the question of evil and suffering. Man's inhumanity to man, at times, has known no bounds. When great injustices have been perpetrated, and no remedy seems to be in sight, the only hope left has been that one day there would be a divine reckoning. Thankfully, John's revelation includes this great hope for those who have suffered much at the hands of others:

> I saw a great white throne and the one sitting on it. The earth and sky fled from his presence, but they found no place to hide. I saw the dead, both great and small, standing before God's throne. And the books were opened, including the Book of Life. And the dead were judged according to what they had done, as recorded in the books. The sea gave up its dead, and death and the grave gave up their dead. And all were judged according to their deeds. Then death and the grave were thrown into the lake of fire. This lake of fire is the second death. And anyone whose name was not found recorded in the Book of Life was thrown into the lake of fire.[9]

John is very clear—the books that contain an account of all the hatred, betrayal, injustice, and unspeakable deeds done by everyone who has ever lived will be opened. Think about it like this. Everyone's life story is going to be posted on an eternal Facebook account. Everything will be exposed, and everything will be made right. Everyone will be held accountable for their life by the Lord of creation. Justice and judgment will be meted out for everyone except those whose names are written in the Book of Life. And the only reason they escape is that their guilt and judgment were borne by Christ upon the cross and they have appropriated his great grace through their faith in him.

It Includes a Mind-Blowing After Party!

As the apostle Paul notes, "No eye has seen, no ear has heard, and no mind has imagined what God has prepared for those who love him."[10] This being the case, the only way that words can begin to approximate how glorious and jaw-dropping the celebration of God's win will be is by using word pictures. John uses the imagery of a wedding:

> Then I heard again what sounded like the shout of a vast crowd or the roar of mighty ocean waves or the crash of loud thunder:
> "Praise the LORD!
> For the Lord our God, the Almighty, reigns.
> Let us be glad and rejoice
> and let us give honor to him.
> For the time has come for the wedding feast of the Lamb,
> and his bride has prepared herself."[11]

Jesus is the groom. His church, those who have trusted him, are his bride. And the ceremony is now over. It's time to get the party started. Eating and drinking, feasting and dancing, storytelling and remembering will go on for days! Who is included? Those who are on the guest list of course—those whose names are written in the Book of Life because they responded to the invitation and said yes to Jesus. If this sounds like your kind of party, the invitation is still open. In the final verses of the Revelation we read these words, "The Spirit and the bride say, 'Come.' Let anyone who hears this say, 'Come.' Let anyone who is thirsty come. Let anyone who desires drink freely from the water of life."[12]

AND IT CHANGES EVERYTHING

"The one sitting on the throne said, 'Look, I am making everything new!'"[13]

Creation Will Be Renewed

Sometimes our view of God's Great Story is so human centered that we exclude the rest of God's creation. As an old hymn reminds us, "There is a wideness in God's mercy."[14] That is, at the end of time, God has a much larger vision of what is going to be made new than most of us. Paul the apostle hints at this in his letter to the believers in Rome:

> For all creation is waiting eagerly for that future day when
> God will reveal who his children really are. Against its will, all
> creation was subjected to God's curse. But with eager hope,
> the creation looks forward to the day when it will join God's
> children in glorious freedom from death and decay.[15]

John's revelation picks up this theme:

> Then I saw a new heaven and a new earth, for the old heaven and
> the old earth had disappeared. And the sea was also gone. And I
> saw the holy city, the new Jerusalem, coming down from God out
> of heaven like a bride beautifully dressed for her husband.[16]

J.R.R. Tolkien portrays this hope beautifully in his storytelling. Christopher

J.H. Wright, in his book *The God I Don't Understand,* revels in this promise of all creation being renewed:

> Did you see the Lord of the Rings trilogy of movies? I went to all three, and I remember the crowds lining up to see Part 3. In fact, whether we'd read the book or not, we all knew how the story would end—with "The Return of the King." Well, we have read God's book, and we also know how the story of the universe will end. It ends with the return of the King and the salvation, not just of "the shire," but of the whole of creation and all God's redeemed humanity from every nation on the planet.[17]

Contrary to what you may have heard, we aren't going to be carted off to some all-inclusive heavenly Club Med in another parsec of the universe. Heaven and earth are going to be made new. Oceans and rivers will be crystal clear, skies will be brilliantly blue, the land will bear its fruit without hindrance, and God's creatures will nobly and peacefully rule the earth.

Reality Will Be Reordered

Isaiah foreshadows how the final chapter of God's Great Story will result in a reordering of all things. Armies will take to farming instead of fighting. Weapons will no longer be instruments of death, but tools for life. Nations will reconcile with each other, and their resources will be invested in the common good. Wolves will hang out with lambs and no wool will fly. Leopards will curl up with baby goats for an afternoon nap. Hurt people will stop hurting other people and the earth will be filled to the brim with people who know and love God.[18]

John's revelation echoes Isaiah's prophecy: "'He will wipe every tear from their eyes. There will be no more death' or mourning or crying or pain, for the *old order of things* has passed away."[19] Have you ever wondered what a new order of things might look like? Will time still exist? Will God's presence be visible to us 24/7? Will God's will always be done? Will the link between cause and effect be broken? Will we still be limited by gravity or will we be able to move effortlessly through the heavens and the earth? When it comes to relationships, will we know one another? Will it be possible to have deep and meaningful relationships with everyone? These are just a few of the questions that begin to come to light when we think about the possibility of a brand-new order!

We Will Be Resurrected and Receive New Bodies

If you have watched your body betray you with age, cancer, or a neurological condition—or laid a parent or spouse or child to rest way too soon—or struggled with chronic pain, or had to bear the weighty responsibility of a body and mind imperfectly formed in the womb, this promise may be your greatest hope. The apostle Paul boldly asserts that...

> it will happen in a moment, in the blink of an eye, when the last trumpet is blown. For when the trumpet sounds, those who have died will be raised to live forever. And we who are living will also be transformed. For our dying bodies must be transformed into bodies that will never die; our mortal bodies must be transformed into immortal bodies.[20]

This hope has been mine since I (Jim) was a small child. My father lost his leg in an oil field explosion when I was still in utero. While he recovered and became a courageous husband and father, there were many things that we could never do together. One day when my mom sensed that I was struggling with the limitations of Dad's condition, she told me of this promise, "One day, Jim, when your dad is in heaven, he will have two good legs." I held tightly to this hope while I was growing up. One day when dad was getting older, I asked him, "What are you going to do when you get to heaven?" I'll never forget his answer: "I'm going to run, and run, till I can't run anymore."

I had the privilege of being with my dad when he passed away several years ago. When the nurses turned off his life support and he passed from this life, the first thing that came to my mind was the fulfillment of this enduring hope that had sustained our whole family for the fifty-six years he lived in his broken body. The only goodbye that seemed appropriate was to whisper, "Run, Dad, run!"

Your story may be different in detail, but it is the same in substance. We, and everyone we know and love, live in a body that is frail, vulnerable, and will ultimately perish. But in Jesus's resurrection and return we have the hope of all hopes—a brand-new life and a new spiritual body that will equip us for all eternity. In the end God wins and so do we!

OUR STORY

BECAUSE GOD WINS,
WE CAN LIVE WITH CONFIDENCE

That's the purpose of Revelation. It is God's timeless reminder that he is still sovereign. No matter what we are facing here and now we can move forward with great confidence because we know the ending!

I (Jim) am an avid Baylor football fan. So much so, that I spring for season tickets and attend every game I can. When they play on the road, though, I often have to record the game and watch it later when I get home from our Saturday night worship service. At first, I tried to keep the final score a secret, but I would get multiple texts revealing the outcome of the game, or I would inadvertently see the score when checking something else on my phone. So I gave up and started checking the score when I had a chance and it changed the way I experienced a game.

If we lost, I wouldn't watch the replay when I got home because I didn't want to put myself through all the tension and disappointment. But if we won, I loved watching the game on tape almost as much as being there in person. Why? When I knew the outcome, it changed how I looked at every fumble, interception, or stupid penalty. When you are at the game watching in real time, each one of those things is painful and frustrating to experience because they may indeed lead to losing the game. You live and die with every miscue and bad play. But when I know how the game ends, I don't panic, or despair, or become anxious about any of those things because I know that in the end my team wins!

As you read this book you may be facing a job loss, divorce, moral failure, catastrophic illness, or child gone prodigal. Whatever it is, though, there is no need to panic or despair. This choice or event does not have the power to ultimately define or defeat you. Because everything gets resolved and redeemed in the end, you can live with more confidence and hope in the present!

BECAUSE GOD WINS, WE CAN LIVE WITH PURPOSE IN THIS LIFE AND THE NEXT!

Near the end of Matthew's account of Jesus's life, he records three of Jesus's parables that deal with the end of the world as we know it. One of those is traditionally known as the parable of the talents. More recently it is referred to as the parable of the three servants.[21]

In Jesus's story a master who is about to embark on a long trip entrusts large portions of his estate to three servants. For the sake of our modern ears, let's say to one he entrusts 50 percent of his estate, to the second 20 percent, and to the third a 10 percent share.

He does not tell them how to invest their shares of his estate, only that he will come back someday, and they will have to give an account of how they managed what they had been given. The first and second servants, applying all that they had learned and observed from their master, doubled their shares. The third servant had a different take on the character of the master, so in fear, he buried his 10 percent.

At the end of the story, the master returns. The first two servants joyfully reveal how they had doubled the shares they had been given. The master then affirms and blesses them, saying, "Well done, my good and faithful servants. You have been faithful in handling this small amount, so now I will give you many more responsibilities. Let's celebrate together!"[22] Things did not go as well for the third servant. Let's just say he loses everything he had been entrusted with and gets kicked to the curb by his master.

Don't miss this. This is a parable that provides a window into the future after God wraps everything up at Jesus's return. Two things are promised. One is what we expect, but the second may come as a surprise. First, he invites his servants into a celebration, and it will be big—picture a Jewish wedding on steroids! And second, the one you may find surprising, is that he says, "Come on in and I will give you even more responsibilities!" Huh?

For all of you who have thought eternity would be just one extremely long church service and frankly lost interest, Jesus has really good news for you. God is going to let us help him manage and care for the new heavens and the new earth just like he planned for us to do at the dawn of creation. Only this time, there will be no serpent in the garden. He will welcome us to be cocreators and managers of his heavenly, infinite estate and join him in writing new stories of his redeeming love in all of creation. According to Jesus, eternity is going to be active, progressing, and purposeful beyond our comprehension. It's hard to beat Dallas Willard's description of what lies in store for those who trust Jesus:

> Our destiny is to join a tremendously creative team effort, under unimaginably splendid leadership, on an inconceivably vast plane of activity, with ever more comprehensive cycles of productivity and enjoyment.[23]

Whatever you do, don't miss it! Live your one and only life in a way that one day when the Master returns you will hear him say to you, "Well done, my good and faithful servant. You have been faithful in handling this small amount, so now I will give you many more responsibilities. Let's celebrate together!"[24]

FINDING YOUR PLACE

We hope our telling of God's Great Story has made you curious about God and what he is up to in our crazy world. We also hope we have helped you think about God more clearly. Even though we've come to the end of our book, this is not the end of God's story. As a matter of fact, we believe he is writing new chapters right now all over the world in the lives of billions of people who trust him. How cool is that!

And here's the really good news. God wants to include you. He has a special role for you in his story—a role that only you can play. Does that sound exciting? Does it sound scary? Does it sound like both? That's all okay! Some people are immediately stoked to hear that God has a special mission for them to accomplish with their life. But others hear the big news and respond just like Moses did when God called him:

"God, you can't mean me."

"I think you've got the wrong person."

"No one knows who I am."

"There must be someone who could do a better job than me."

If these thoughts are in your way, keeping you from finding your place in God's Great Story, we want to share with you one final thread that runs through every chapter you have just read. It is a secret message that will encourage you and bring you hope for a bright future—God surprises.

Here's what we mean. In every chapter, God chooses and uses people and circumstances that we normally wouldn't expect. He turns things upside down. He flips the script. He taps people on the shoulder—the "wrong" people, from a human perspective—and invites them to be the lead in a crucial part of the story. Check this out:

- An Almighty God could have created people as robots, programming them to do everything he wants all the time. Instead, he gives people, his special creation, the freedom to say yes or no to him, to follow him or turn their backs on him.

- God chose Abraham and Sarah, a childless couple way past childbearing age, to start a new tribe and nation of people.

- God called Moses to come out of retirement and lead God's people out of slavery in Egypt. Moses was way more comfortable watching sheep roam the desert than leading a million stubborn people through it.

- God picked David—the youngest son of Jesse, not the oldest—to be Israel's second king and forgave him when he made bad moral decisions that hurt himself and others.

- The prophets were a mixed bag of strange misfits whom God used to clarify his expectations and purposes for his people and to warn them to shape up or get ready to ship out.

- Jesus, God's Son and the King of kings, was not born in a palace of privilege but in a borrowed stable. He came to establish God's Kingdom and rule on earth, but he didn't do it by the power of the sword, coercing people to follow him. Instead, he wooed people with the power of sacrificial love.

- Paul, the first missionary, was a super-spreader of the good news of Jesus. But before that, he tried to silence the message of Jesus by persecuting and killing those who were following him.

- And someday, even when most people will seem to be rejecting the message of Jesus and turning the world into one big dumpster fire, God will pull the biggest surprise of all by sending Jesus back to the earth to clean up the mess. Jesus will make all things right and all things new.

Do you feel the puzzle pieces clicking together? God's MO is not using people who have Marvel-like superpowers. Instead, he finds ordinary people who are more likely to have super flaws. How surprising is that?

Everyone—no matter how young or old, rich or poor; no matter where they live, how they look, or what they've done—everyone is invited to find their place in God's story. And that definitely includes you!

So, what will it be? Are you ready for an exciting new chapter in your life? Are you ready to follow Jesus wherever he leads you, no matter your age or stage in your journey? If you are, just whisper a prayer and let him know—then get ready to live out the great, challenging adventure that God has in store for you!

NOTES

THE POWER OF STORY

1. Nancy Duarte, *Resonate: Present Visual Stories that Transform Audiences* (Wiley and Sons, 2010), www.duarte .com; Donald Miller, *Building a StoryBrand: Clarify Your Message So Customers Will Listen* (Harper Collins Leadership, 2017), www.storybrand.com.

CHAPTER 1: GOD CREATES

1. See Genesis 12.

2. Psalm 139:13-16 NIV.

3. Genesis 1:1.

4. See 2 Kings 25 and 2 Chronicles 36.

5. If it bothers you that God may not have created everything in one historical week, then ask yourself this question: "Does it bother me that God doesn't create a baby instantaneously, but designed the nine-month process we call pregnancy?" God is free to create as God chooses. Sometimes it happens quickly; at other times it takes longer. We believe that Genesis 1 points to an unlimited amount of time in which God created everything.

6. Genesis 1:3-5.

7. Genesis 1:6-8.

8. Genesis 1:9-13.

9. Genesis 1:14-19.

10. Genesis 1:20-23.

11. Genesis 1:24-31.

12. Genesis 2:1-3.

13. Genesis 1:26-28.

14. Genesis 2:18,21-24.

15. Colossians 1:15-16.

16. Genesis 1:28.

17. Elahe Isadi, "The Powerful words of forgiveness delivered to Dylann Roof by victims' relatives," *Washington Post*, June 19, 2015, https://www.washingtonpost.com/news/post-nation/wp/2015/06/19/hate-wont-win-the -powerful-words-delivered-to-dylann-roof-by-victims-relatives/.

CHAPTER 2: GOD BLESSES

1. You can read the official version in Genesis 12–25.

2. David Brooks, *The Second Mountain* (New York: Random House, 2019), 55.

3. Genesis 12:1-3.

4. Genesis 12:2-3.

5. Walter Brueggemann, *Genesis: Interpretation: A Bible Commentary for Teaching and Preaching* (Atlanta, GA: John Knox Press, 1982), 37.

6. Matthew 10:8 NIV; John 13:34 NIV; Ephesians 4:32 NIV.

7. Genesis 12:4-7.

8. Romans 4; Hebrews 11:8-19.

9. Genesis 21:1-7.

10. Galatians 3:6-9.

CHAPTER 3: GOD RESCUES

1. Exodus 1:11,13-14.

2. Although Pharaoh would never have heard of these modern words, he is guilty of anti-Semitism, infanticide, and attempted genocide. Anti-Semitism is an attitude of hostility toward Semites (Jews). It always leads to hostile actions. Infanticide is the action of killing infants. Genocide is the action of destroying a race of people. All three occur while the Israelites are stuck in Egypt. Pharaoh targets a particular race, the Hebrews, and devises a plan to extinguish them. His scheme is to wipe out the entire Jewish nation. This is the first instance of harsh anti-Semitism in the Bible. Sadly, it is not the last. See the story of Haman in Esther 3:6-9 and the story of Herod in Matthew 2:16-17.

3. Peter Kreeft and Ronald K. Tacelli, *Handbook of Christian Apologetics: Hundreds of Answers to Crucial Questions* (Downers Grove, IL: InterVarsity Press, 1994), Kindle locations 1391-92.

4. Rick Warren, "God's Plan for Your Pain," PastorRick.com (blog), July 11, 2018, https://pastorrick.com/gods-plan-for-your-pain/.

5. Exodus 3:1-8.

6. Exodus 3:10.

7. Romans 8:29 NIV.

8. Exodus 9:13-16.

9. Exodus 14:10-14.

10. Exodus 19:1-4.

11. Exodus 19:5-6.

12. Genesis 12:2-3.

13. Exodus 20:1-17.

CHAPTER 4: GOD CHOOSES

1. You can read about Saul's foibles in 1 Samuel 9–15.

2. David's story is quite extensive and engaging and can be found in 1 Samuel 16–31; 2 Samuel 1–23; 1 Kings 1–2; 1 Chronicles 11–29.

3. 1 Samuel 13:14 KJV.

4. Carolyn Custis James, *Malestrom* (Grand Rapids, MI: Zondervan, 2015), 80.

5. Walter Brueggemann, *Genesis: Interpretation: A Bible Commentary for Teaching and Preaching* (Atlanta, GA: John Knox Press, 1982), 209.

6. Genesis 15–21; 27; 37; Luke 15:11-31; Matthew 20:16 KJV.

7. 2 Samuel 16:5-14; 19:15-23; 1 Kings 2:1-12.

8. Aleksandr Solzhenitsyn, *The Gulag Archipelago* (New York: Harper & Row, 1974), 168.

9. 2 Samuel 7:12-16.

10. 1 Samuel 16:7.

11. 1 Samuel 17:34-37.

12. 1 Samuel 17:43.

13. Hebrews 11:6 NIV.

14. 2 Samuel 11:1-27.

15. This iconic phrase comes from the Watergate affair that led to the downfall of President Richard Nixon.

16. 2 Samuel 12:1-25.

17. Psalm 51:1-4,7,10-13,16-17.

18. Psalm 139:1-6.

19. Romans 7:18-19,24.

20. Acts 13:36 NIV.

CHAPTER 5: GOD WARNS

1. Many commentators date the split of Israel around 930 BC, but the exact date is debated. For the sake of clarity, I will assume the 930 BC date.

2. Esv.org/resources/esv-global-study-bible/facts-ezra-7/.

3. Gordon Fee, *How to Read the Bible for All Its Worth* (Grand Rapids, MI: Zondervan, 2003), 182.

4. I have not listed Daniel or Lamentations as among the prophetic works because in the Hebrew Bible they are classified as Writings.

5. Christopher J.H. Wright, *How to Preach and Teach the Old Testament for All Its Worth* (Grand Rapids, MI: Zondervan, 2016), 186.

6. Jeremiah 15:18.

7. Hosea 4:1-3.

8. Jeremiah 3:12-13,15.

9. Jeremiah 7:3-7.

10. Christopher J.H. Wright, *How to Preach and Teach the Old Testament for All Its Worth* (Grand Rapids, MI: Zondervan, 2016), 208.

11. Jeremiah 31:3.

12. Jeremiah 31:1-6.

13. Isaiah 5:4. This small parable is found in verses 1-7.

14. Isaiah 9:6-7.

15. Hebrews 8:7-13.

16. Thomas R. Schreiner, *Ten Things You Should Know about the Biblical Covenants.* Crossway, July 17, 2017, https://www.crossway.org/articles/10-things-you-should-know-about-the-biblical-covenants/.

17. Hosea 2:14-15.

18. Hosea 3:5.

CHAPTER 6: GOD SAVES

1. Matthew 1:21 NIV.

2. Galatians 4:4.

3. God's covenant people were originally called Israelites. They weren't called Jews (from the word "Judea") until they were exiled to Babylon in 587/586 BC and later returned to the Promised Land. Today we say that adherents of Israel's faith are Jews. Jews who live in modern Israel call themselves Israelis.

4. Mark 1:14 NIV.

5. Phillips Brooks, "O Little Town of Bethlehem."

6. Mark 1:11 NIV.

7. Mark 1:14-15.

8. Matthew 4:18-19.

9. Matthew 8:23-27.

10. Matthew 8:1-4.

11. See Mark 5:1-20.

12. See Mark 5:21-24,35-43.

13. Jesus can be seen so much as Savior that his other roles are marginalized. Dallas Willard rightly laments "the absence of Jesus the teacher from our lives. Strangely, we seem prepared to learn how to live from almost anyone but him…The disappearance of Jesus as teacher explains why today in Christian churches—of whatever leaning—little effort is made to teach people to do what he did and taught…We do not seriously consider Jesus as our teacher on how to live, hence we cannot think of ourselves, in our moment-to-moment existence, as his students or disciples" (Dallas A. Willard, *The Divine Conspiracy*, [New York: HarperCollins, 1997], 55-57).

14. Matthew 7:12.

15. Luke 15:1-7.

16. Luke 15:8-10.

17. Luke 15:11-32.

18. The account of Jesus's last week comprises between 25 and 50 percent of the four Gospels. Clearly, they are written primarily to tell this part of his story.

19. Matthew 21:13 NIV.

20. Luke 23:34.

21. Luke 23:43.

22. John 19:26-27.

23. Mark 15:34.

24. John 19:28.

25. John 19:30.

26. Luke 23:46.

27. Matthew 26:39.

28. Dallas A. Willard, *The Divine Conspiracy* (New York: HarperCollins, 1997), 64.

29. See, for example, Romans 5:8; 8:34; 2 Corinthians 5:14; 1 Thessalonians 5:10.

CHAPTER 7: GOD SENDS

1. Acts 1:8.

2. Acts 7:54–8:1.

3. Galatians 1:13 NIV.

4. Paraphrased from Acts 9:1-15.

5. Acts 13:1-4.

6. See Acts 13–14.

7. See Acts 16–18.

8. See Acts 19–21.

9. Acts 20:22-24.

10. Mac and Mary Owen, *Never Let Go* (Lucas Lane, 2013).

11. Dr. Seuss, *Oh the Places You'll Go* (New York: Random House Books for Young Readers, 1990).

12. "Mother Teresa," Biography, April 27, 2017, https://www.biography.com/religious-figure/mother-teresa.

13. "Francis S. Collins, M.D., Ph.D.," American Academy of Achievement, https://achievement.org/achiever/francis-s-collins/.

14. "An Interview with Dallas Willard," www.dwillard.org/about.

CHAPTER 8: GOD WINS

1. J.R.R. Tolkien, *The Lord of the Rings* (New York: Houghton Mifflin, 1994), 997.

2. Matthew 24; Mark 13; Luke 21:5-36.

3. 1 Corinthians 15:52.

4. "Eucatastrophe" is a word coined by J.R.R. Tolkien. He combines the Greek prefix "eu," which means good,

with the word "catastrophe." Thus, it is a tragic event which actually becomes the source of some kind of redeeming good. Tolkien develops this idea in his essay "On Fairy-Stories," presented as the Andrew Lang Lecture at the University of St. Andrews, Scotland, 1939; first published in *Essays Presented to Charles Williams*, ed. C. S. Lewis, Oxford University Press, 1947.

5. Revelation 17:3-6.

6. Revelation 5:4-10.

7. Luke 23:34.

8. 2 Thessalonians 2:8.

9. Revelation 20:11-15.

10. 1 Corinthians 2:9.

11. Revelation 19:6-7.

12. Revelation 22:17.

13. Revelation 21:5.

14. Frederick William Faber, "There's a Wideness in God's Mercy," 1862.

15. Romans 8:19-21.

16. Revelation 21:1-2.

17. Christopher J.H. Wright, *The God I Don't Understand: Reflections on Tough Questions of Faith* (Grand Rapids, MI: Zondervan, 2008), 179.

18. Isaiah 2:2,4; 11:6-9.

19. Revelation 21:4 NIV, emphasis added.

20. 1 Corinthians 15:52-53.

21. Matthew 25:14-30.

22. Matthew 25:21,23.

23. Dallas Willard, *The Divine Conspiracy: Rediscovering Our Hidden Life in God* (San Francisco: Harper San Francisco, 1997), 399.

24. Matthew 25:21,23.

ACKNOWLEDGMENTS

Our hearts are full of thanks for the people who helped this book come into existence.

It all began as a sermon series at Preston Trail Community Church. A gifted team of ministers thinks creatively and artistically about what goes into our worship services every week. They also shape every new series that rolls out. We want to single out two staff members who have been our ministry partners for more than fifteen years and who especially influenced the evolution of the series before it became a book: Allison Harrell, creative pastor, who wrote "The Story Between the Story" to introduce each new message; and Warren Jacobs, worship pastor, who envisioned the potential impact of this series from the very beginning. Kudos also go to Devon Laird, who graphically illustrated weekly videos that brought "The Story Between the Story" to life. The genius of these three lives on in this book.

Next it became an idea in the mind and heart of Bob Hawkins Jr., president of Harvest House Publishers. On a trip to meet new authors back in 2018, Bob met with us to congratulate us on our first book, *Tough Stuff Parenting*, which Harvest House had just published. At the end of our time together, Bob asked, "Do you guys have anything in mind for a next book?" Jim mentioned a series we had preached a few years earlier entitled "God's Big Story." Bob was immediately intrigued. When the prez is interested, momentum builds. Soon we were in Eugene, Oregon, visualizing and storyboarding what would eventually become *Finding Your Place in God's Great Story*. What a treat to spend an entire day working with Barb Sherrill, Kyle Hatfield, and Gene Skinner on the project. When the day was over, Harvest House committed to three books—one for preteens, one for littles, and one for adults and teens. We are truly grateful to the Harvest House team for their partnership with us in helping every generation find their place in God's great story!

As always, we offer a special thanks to our lovely wives, Robin Archinal Johnson and Denise O'Brien Basden, for their partnership in the gospel from the beginning.